WRITTEN BY A SMALL GROUP

J. ALEX KIRK • JAY ANDERSON

MYRON CROCKETT • ÚNA LUCEY-LEE

JANICE McWILLIAMS • TINA TENG • SANDRA VAN OPSTAL

SMALL GROUP

NEW EDITION

LEADERS' HANDBOOK

DEVELOPING TRANSFORMATIONAL COMMUNITIES

IVP Connect

An imprint of InterVarsity Press
Downers Grove, Illinois

InterVarsity Press
P.O. Box 1400, Downers Grove, IL 60515-1426
World Wide Web: www.ivpress.com
E-mail: email@ivpress.com

InterVarsity Press® is the book-publishing division of InterVarsity Christian Fellowship/ USA®, a movement of students and faculty active on campus at hundreds of universities, colleges and schools of nursing in the United States of America, and a member movement of the International Fellowship of Evangelical Students. For information about local and regional activities, write Public Relations Dept., InterVarsity Christian Fellowship/USA, 6400 Schroeder Rd., P.O. Box 7895, Madison, WI 53707-7895, or visit the IVCF website at <www.intervarsity.org>.

All Scripture quotations, unless otherwise indicated, are taken from the Holy Bible, New International Version®. NIV®. Copyright ©1973, 1978, 1984 by International Bible Society. Used by permission of Zondervan Publishing House. All rights reserved.

Design: Cindy Kiple

ISBN 978-0-8308-2112-9

Printed in the United States of America ∞

 InterVarsity Press is committed to protecting the environment and to the responsible use of natural resources. As a member of Green Press Initiative we use recycled paper whenever possible. To learn more about the Green Press Initiative, visit <www.greenpressinitiative.org>.

Library of Congress Cataloging-in-Publication Data

Small group leaders' handbook: developing transformational
communities / J. Alex Kirk . . . [et al.].
    p. cm.
Includes bibliographical references.
ISBN 978-0-8308-2112-9 (pbk.: alk. paper)
1. Church group work. 2. Small groups—Religious
aspects—Christianity. I. Kirk, J. Alex.
BV652.2.S575 2009
253'.7—dc22

                                                            2009031646

| P | 20 | 19 | 18 | 17 | 16 | 15 | 14 | 13 | 12 | 11 | 10 | 9 | 8 | 7 | 6 | 5 |
| Y | 25 | 24 | 23 | 22 | 21 | 20 | 19 | 18 | 17 | 16 | 15 | 14 |

CONTENTS

A NOTE FROM THE PUBLISHER

INTERVARSITY CHRISTIAN FELLOWSHIP has long seen small groups as central to discipleship and evangelism. Small groups, the reasoning goes, provide people with a secure base of relationships; from there they're free to explore the bold claims of Christianity, to gain insight into how the truths of the Bible speak into their everyday lives, and to experience firsthand the love of God communicated through the ministry of his people. In small groups we borrow wisdom from each other, and we offer the love of Christ to one another.

Sounds great, right? Try leading one.

Recognizing the challenges that small group leaders face— particularly when they first enter into leadership—a team of InterVarsity staff came together in the early 1980s and drafted what became the original *Small Group Leaders' Handbook.* The book was used widely by churches and parachurch ministries for more than a decade, when the authors handed off the mantle to a new group. Led by Jimmy Long, who participated in the first edition and went on to write the widely influential book on postmodern ministry *Generating Hope,* the second edition addressed the changes to leadership necessary in light of the generational changes that had taken place, and emphasized four core values that would set the agenda for group life once again: community, nurture, worship and prayer, and outreach.

The time came once again to reconsider what we mean by small groups, and how we cultivate those values in a group setting. And so, at Jimmy Long's behest, a new crop of people were gathered who are passionate about the potential that can be found in each small group that calls itself Christian: the potential for transformational communities that transform communities with the gospel of Christ.

Some of our seven contributors to this entirely new, third edition of *Small Group Leaders' Handbook* knew each other long before they entered into this writing project. But thanks to the spirit in which they undertook this project, they've all come to know one another well. They met together regularly, both in person and—something the contributors to previous editions can't claim—online and via e-mail. And they studied the Bible together, prayed together, and through their work on this project participated in God's mission together—which is to see more and more people reconciled to God and to one another. So in the writing of this book as much as in what is written in this book there is evidence that God can do wonderful things for and through people who are willing to take the challenge of developing transformational communities in the name of Christ.

Maybe you're willing to take that challenge too. If so, may this book be a blessing to you.

ABOUT THE AUTHORS

J. ALEX KIRK is the team leader for the *Small Group Leaders'
Handbook.* He is on staff with InterVarsity Christian Fellowship at UNC-Chapel Hill.

JANICE McWILLIAMS provides staff training and spiritual for-
mation for InterVarsity Christian Fellowship in the Mid-Atlantic
region.

SANDRA VAN OPSTAL and her husband live in inner-city Chicago, where she directs InterVarsity's Urban Program. She
leads the Urbana Student Mission Conference worship team
and serves on the national leadership team for the Latino ministry La Fe.

MYRON CROCKETT was an InterVarsity staffworker for nine
years at University of New Orleans and Tulane University. The
former director of the Katrina Relief Urban Plunge, he is now a
graduate student at Trinity Evangelical Divinity School. He
lives in the Chicago area with his wife and daughter.

ÚNA LUCEY-LEE is an area director for InterVarsity. While working on this book project, she moved from her native California
to the Chicago area, where she lives with her husband.

TINA TENG is an InterVarsity staffworker with Harvard-Rad-
cliffe Christian Fellowship, and a Harvard chaplain.

JAY ANDERSON is a senior campus staff worker for InterVarsity at the University of Wisconsin–Eau Claire. He lives with
his wife and kids in Eau Claire.

1

1106

THE STORY OF A TRANSFORMATIONAL COMMUNITY

J. Alex Kirk

TWO WORDS describe my first two years of ministry experience: utter failure.

I graduated from the University of North Carolina, a traditional campus complete with all the trimmings: great basketball, a gorgeous Southern-style campus, and all the joys and tribulations of dorm life. My experiences as a student in our 250-person InterVarsity Christian Fellowship chapter shaped me in profound ways—particularly my understanding of the value and centrality of community. Small group Bible studies were the foundation of community for our chapter. Investing my life in an authentic and intentional community over the course of four years in small groups radically transformed my character and my understanding of the gospel. I was sold. As I wrapped up my senior year I applied to be a campus minister with InterVarsity.

I was given the task of working by myself at Virginia Commonwealth University, a commuter campus in Richmond, Virginia. VCU was a large, urban university known less for its football team (it had none) and more for its art department (complete with all *those* trimmings: multicolored hair, tattoos and piercings where I had never seen piercings before). I knew nothing about art—even my stick-figures were ugly. Nevertheless, more than one person told me that the VCU students were lucky to have me, and I was rather inclined to agree with them. I was sure that I was ready to plunge into my first assignment.

When I arrived at VCU, the InterVarsity chapter was a healthy and thriving fellowship of fifty students. By the end of my second year on campus, we were down to fifteen. I tried everything, but nothing could stop our free-fall. The chapter was dying and I had killed it. In my darker moments, I considered looking into whether or not Wal-Mart greeters received decent health benefits.

Frustrated was the word that described me best for much of those first two years. I struggled to understand the campus culture. As my feelings of failure grew, so, too, did my need for self-justification. I couldn't stop privately comparing my experience as a student at UNC with what I considered to be an inferior student experience at VCU. I was alternately full of despair and pride. Instead of learning to love the people to whom God had sent me, I was railing against them.

Student life on a commuter campus is fragmented. Over 80 percent of the VCU students did not live on campus in residence halls. On top of a full academic course load, many of them worked from ten to forty hours a week. On school days they got in their cars, drove to campus, parked, went to class, got back in their cars and left for the day. That was the extent of their interaction with life on campus.

Our chapter reflected the scattered student lifestyle. One of our small group leaders lived forty-five minutes from campus. I had learned as a student that authentic and vibrant community was the operating system of a healthy campus ministry—that apart from holy relationships there could be no holy outcomes. In my experience, small groups formed the heartbeat of this kind of community. But who had time for small groups, holy relationships or dynamic community at VCU?

Near the end of my second year I gave a desperate talk at our Thursday night "large" group. We looked at Mark 6, the story of Jesus feeding the five thousand. One tiny detail recorded by Mark captured my imagination: "Then Jesus directed them [the disciples] to have all the people sit down in groups on the green grass" (Mark 6:39). The people complied, and Jesus proceeded to miraculously feed them.

I proposed to the students who were returning the next year that we needed "a patch of green grass" to call our own. We needed a home base, a hub, a center. We needed our own patch of green grass in the middle of the city. I asked them to consider what it might look like if our community had a place where we might gather together to be fed by Jesus. I asked them to choose to make proximity to campus a priority in their living decisions for the next year.

Chris, Emmanuel, Joel and Steve—who made up the majority of our dwindling men's small group Bible study—were in the room that evening. They had been talking about living together the next year in an off-campus apartment. The Lord captured their hearts with the vision of creating a patch of green grass for our chapter. They spent several weeks looking for apartments, dismissing anything further than walking distance from campus. Eventually, God gave them (and us) 1106 Grove Avenue, Apartment 1, half a block off campus. It even had a decent-sized living room—big enough for us, anyway. So the next fall we moved our men's small group and our Thursday night gathering into the living room of 1106.

And that fall, from God-only-knows-where, people came.

Students met at 1106 for small group Bible studies during the week and gathered for worship on Thursday nights. On weekends people showed up unannounced and were welcomed. Impromptu parties popped up with great regularity. The Tuesday night men's small group morphed from a one-hour Bible study "meeting" to a Bible study plus after-party that ran into the early morning hours (most often involving video games). On Thursday nights we filled the living room, overflowed into the kitchen, down the hall and onto open window sills. From one small group, the Lord was rebuilding an entire community.

One weekend our patch of green grass hosted what became our annual root beer keg party. Much to my students' delight, it was broken up by the police (his exact words: "You guys are kind of loud . . . and I *know* that's not root beer!").

All year long "1106" in our vernacular meant a place that was home. But it was more than a place; it was a group of people, a transformational community, a glorious juxtaposition of activity and rest, of retreat and energy, of welcoming in and sending out. Chris, Emmanuel, Joel and Steve worked hard to make it that way. And as this small group of men worked to bless other people, they themselves were blessed. In their small group community they learned conflict, forgiveness, encouragement, accountability, long-suffering and the joy of being a part of God's mission in community. The guys at 1106 provided the physical space and the relational synergy to build a larger greenhouse of community where many lives were changed. On a campus fraught with commuter-driven isolation, loneliness and fragmentation, the Spirit used this small group of men and a little patch of green grass to create holy ground and a holy community of his people. Our community popped with vibrancy, energy and welcome.

We ended that year having grown from fifteen to fifty-five. The next year we found a spot on campus to meet, and we grew from fifty-five to ninety. The next year we grew from ninety to 140. The growth went beyond numbers: addictions were broken; artists learned to use their gifts to bless others for the glory of God; people far from God were brought near to him. We built relationships with fraternities and sororities and partnered in service projects. We built relationships with cultural groups and participated in interracial dialogues. We painted ourselves silver and did ridiculous outreach events on campus. Later we helped launch a new ministry at VCU to reach out to a specific community on campus, and they saw tremendous growth and fruit. Dozens of other patches of green grass were planted, so that several generations of small group leaders would point back to 1106 as a critical part of their spiritual journey. All of this out of one small group of four guys.

I tore up the Wal-Mart application.

THE VISION FOR TRANSFORMATIONAL COMMUNITIES

From one small group of twelve disciples, Jesus launched a movement that changed the world. He's still changing the world through the legacy of that first small group, and he's doing it in part through the ministry of small groups. We want to invite you to join in this movement. We want to prepare you to lead a small group.

Here's what we mean when we say "small group":

A small group is a transformational community that studies the Bible, prays and participates in God's mission together for the purposes of God's transforming work.

Notice that the vision for small groups has transformational community at its center. Not cheap community. Not virtual community. Not what-we-happen-to-have-in-common-at-the-moment community. Not small-talk-in-passing community. Not community when it's convenient. *Transformational* community.

The commuter college campus is not the only place where we find lives devoid of genuine, life-giving relationships. From the cities to the suburbs to the most rural outposts (even and especially on traditional college campuses), there is a pandemic of loneliness and isolation in our culture. That the vast majority of the people in your church or campus or neighborhood or workplace are deeply lonely is one of the most crippling crises of our time.

We were created for community: it is part of what it means to be created in the image of a God-in-relationship: Father, Son, Holy Spirit. These are innately *relational* words. A father must have offspring; a son comes from parents; a spirit is inherent in something or someone. God *is* a relationship. And the world God made reflects his relational nature: grass and geese and planets and water are all specific combinations of relationships between atoms and protons and electrons. Humans likewise are a dizzying combination of relationships: organs and muscles and synapses firing. Our bodies are a web of relationships, and we were made for relationships. That is part of what it means to be made in God's image.

Without a life of healthy, interdependent relationships, we are ill-equipped to answer the most important questions in life: Who am I? Who (or what) is God? What am I doing here? Apart from relationships that encourage and challenge us, we are barely alive.

Transformational community is thus the critical component of any thriving small group. Transformational communities have specific practices, disciplines that create the space for transformation to happen: these involve studying the Scriptures, praying and participating in God's redemptive mission together. We'll take a brief look at each of these disciplines now and unpack them in greater detail in future chapters.

STUDYING THE BIBLE (EVEN ECCLESIASTES)

Bethany was in trouble and she knew it. She had a significant, up-front role in our ministry. But spiritual questions had turned into spiritual struggles that had developed into full-blown spiritual depression. And now Bethany was deep in the pit of despair. Nothing made sense any more: academics, relationships, God.

Complicating the crisis was her Old Testament class. Every Tuesday and Thursday for an hour and fifteen minutes Bethany faced an all-out assault on the trustworthiness and reliability of the stories and the character of God that were presented in the Scriptures. Not only was she emotionally distraught, she was intellectually bewildered. Was it possible to know anything about God at all?

Few people in Bethany's life knew that the only time she could muster up the ability to read Scripture or to pray was when she was in front of three hundred people on Thursday nights. Bethany wasn't pretending that things were fine— actually, she was in near-panic mode. But she was unsure about what to do with her leadership role in the chapter or the vacuum in her life that used to be her soul.

I was one of the few who knew the full story of Bethany's struggles. In spite of our weekly meetings and my fervent prayers, I watched helplessly as she slipped further into the abyss. Eventually it became clear that a number of things had to change. One of those things was that Bethany needed to find a way to reconnect with God in the midst of her struggles.

Second semester, Bethany joined a small group that was just getting started. I was encouraged by her initiative until I heard what book of Scripture they were studying: Ecclesiastes.

In case you haven't been recreationally reading through Ecclesiastes recently, here's how the book *starts*:

The words of the Teacher, son of David, king in Jerusalem:
"Meaningless! Meaningless!"
    says the Teacher.
"Utterly meaningless!
    Everything is meaningless." (Ecclesiastes 1:1-2)

Now I had a new prayer for Bethany: *Please God, protect Bethany from Ecclesiastes.*

While Bethany faithfully attended the small group, the Lord gathered together a community to encourage and pray for her. They shared in her struggles, and together they wrestled with the Scriptures. At the end of the spring semester Bethany was still struggling, but in the midst of the struggle there were a few fresh experiences of clarity. And Ecclesiastes had been a part of it. "Ecclesiastes was good for me," Bethany said as she continued to work through her questions. "I've had to wrestle with the realization that, maybe, apart from God everything *is* meaningless."

Bethany's personal struggles and the challenges of her Old Testament class had disconnected her from God's larger, life-giving story—the only one whose arc and width are large enough to gather up the details of our little stories and make sense of them all. Without God's story to help frame our personal stories, we're like a note wrenched out of a symphony—we still make noise, but without the beauty or purpose that was intended. We do not know God, and we do not know what he is about; consequently, we do not know who we are or what we are to be about.

A small group is a Scripture-centered community where people can regularly be oriented and reoriented as they find their place in the life-giving story of God. We create patches of green grass for people to be fed by the Scriptures, to learn this story as well as to live out of it.

I had to ask the Lord later for forgiveness about the whole "protect her from Ecclesiastes" thing.

A small group is a transformational community that *studies the Bible*, prays and participates in God's mission together for the purposes of God's transforming work.

PRAYER: INTERCEDING OVER TEETER-TOTTERS

After eight years as the InterVarsity staff worker at VCU, I was getting antsy. It felt like it was time to move on, but I wasn't quite sure where to go or what the next step would be. One night in the fall of my ninth year, I received a phone call offering me the opportunity go back to work with InterVarsity at my alma mater, the University of North Carolina.

To my old friends from college the opportunity sounded like a no-brainer, but I wasn't so sure. My wife, Kelly, and I were firmly entrenched in our church and community in Richmond. On top of that, the InterVarsity chapter at UNC was in significant transition. I had four wonderful years as a student there, and nine years after that to over-romanticize my experiences and to conveniently forget all that was painful. What if I went back and things fell apart? What if I repeated my "utter-failure" experience? What if my second time around at UNC tainted my (admittedly) rose-colored-glasses-love for my alma mater? And most important: was God calling us to do this?

As Kelly and I discussed the decision, we'd teeter-totter back and forth. One day I would lean toward going and she would lean toward staying. The next day we'd switch places. After a couple of weeks we were both feeling teeter-totter queasiness. We needed to bring our small group into the decision-making process.

We asked our friends if we could hijack the group for one week to help us make the "do we stay or do we go" decision. We asked them to spend the week praying for us and listening to the Lord on our behalf. We invited them to jot down any questions, insights or thoughts they had as they prayed. At the end of the week we would gather for a time of prayer, question-asking and discernment together.

The next week I was on the "stay" end of the teeter-totter; Kelly was on the "go" end. For over an hour our small group asked us good questions and spent time praying over us. There was no definitive moment that night—no lightning bolt from the sky or angels dancing—but as we closed our time together in prayer, I realized that I had moved, ever so slightly, toward the "go" end of the teeter-totter.

Surprisingly, Kelly *hadn't* moved. We were on the same side for the first time. Over the next couple of weeks our small group continued to pray alongside us. In the end this small group (comprising some of our closest friends in Richmond) blessed us to leave them as they affirmed the decision to go.

Four years later, the rose-colored glasses are a little beat up, but they're still intact.

We live in a fallen world. One of the ramifications of the Fall is that we have to work a little harder to interact with God—to know his will, to hear his voice, to worship him as he deserves. Many times we equate worship only with singing, and prayer requests amount to little more than "Pray for my uncle's sprained big toe."

A small group becomes a transformational community in part when, as we intentionally build trust, we are able to push past relationships-as-usual to a place where we can be radically *known*. But the goal is not just to be known but to usher one another into the presence of Christ—to worship and intercede and listen together for his voice for ourselves, for one another, for our world.

Kelly and I were stuck as we tried to make a major life decision. As we submitted ourselves to the small group community he had given us and invited them to shape our decision, the Lord moved. This is nothing like relationships-as-usual. This is transformational community.

It didn't just happen. It was cultivated through a feedback loop: our willingness to make our decision a communal prayer experience was the result of many months of our group genuinely praying for one another. At the same time, the small group's willingness to engage with our decision continued to deepen our corporate commitment to genuinely pray for one another.

A small group is a transformational community that studies the Bible, *prays* and participates in God's mission together for the purposes of God's transforming work.

PARTICIPATING IN GOD'S MISSION

"I've got to admit, I was starting to wonder what they were

doing with all of this money." Will was a fantastic small group leader for a first-year men's small group. He was recounting his recent spring break trip to Jamaica. Adam, a member of Will's small group, had gone the year before and recruited the small group to go back over spring break. They were doing basic community development and bridge-building: they were building homes and relationships in order to share their faith and connect people in the community to the local church.

"I was doing the math, and it just wasn't adding up," Will continued. "They not only seemed to be charging us a lot for the trip but they also wanted us to bring all this stuff: clothes and tools and duct tape . . . they had this whole list. I have to confess that I was getting a little grumpy."

"And then I got there. And I met the people. And all I could think was, *What else can I give?*"

Mission, as we'll use it in the context of discussing small groups, is a broad word describing any of God's activities to bring restoration, hope, healing and change to our world. God's mission throughout history is the work of restoration— the work of making things right, moving them toward their intended state. This includes reconciling people to himself (evangelism) and to one another. Restoration happens between individuals in ways that are structural, even cosmic in scope: nations, genders, races, socioeconomic groups, neighborhoods and humans to the rest of the created order.

The patch of green grass does not exist solely for itself. It is a place of gathering together, to be sure, but it is also a place of sending, of mobilizing. As God's people, we are called not only to be reconciled to God but to be a part of his reconciling work in the world. Participating in God's mission includes any restoring and reconciling activity—from service projects to evangelistic events. Crosscultural work like Will's trip is a subset of God's mission to bring the hope of the gospel wherever there is ruin in place of peace. The act of participating in God's mission is leaning into the reality that God is already at work. As we join that work we are finding our true calling in the world as Christ's ambassadors—we are living lives that matter.

A small group is a transformational community that studies the Bible, prays and *participates in God's mission* for the purposes of God's transforming work.

ABOUT THIS BOOK

Our hope and prayer is that you will have stories of your own that sound much like the stories above: individual lives changed, communities transformed, the world changed. This book is about helping you to lead these types of small groups.

In order to better serve and equip you, we've gathered together a group of people from all over the country, made up of different ethnicities, ages, backgrounds and passions. We want this handbook to be as helpful and user-friendly in as many different contexts as possible. We will obviously be drawing from the small group ministries that we've seen on various college campuses, but all of us are sold enough on small groups that we've led them in church contexts as well.

We have broken up the responsibilities of a small group leader into seven categories resulting in eight chapters: gathering your small group, building community, studying the Scriptures, praying and worshiping, shepherding a flock, mobilizing for evangelism and service, and identifying and developing future leaders. Community is so central that we gave it twice the space, and a final chapter is included to help you grow and develop personally as a leader. Each of these chapters is a piece of the small group puzzle, and each one is designed to stand alone so that you can reference it later.

The greatest need in the church today is for trained small group leaders. As you read this, people involved in small groups are being changed and becoming change agents all over the world. Jesus inaugurated small groups; the global church is the result of one. Several years ago one small group resurrected a small and dying Christian community on a little part of the world called Virginia Commonwealth University. The 1106 story is just one of the countless stories throughout history of God raising up transformational communities all over the world. But transformational communities don't just magically appear. The call is urgent and relentless: who will lead? Who will take a risk to step out and create a patch of green grass for people to gather together, to be met by the Lord?

We trust if you're reading this that you're heeding that call. We pray that this book equips you for the work ahead.

2

GATHERING A SMALL GROUP

Janice McWilliams

BERT AND SUSIE, a couple of friends at my church, led a small group a couple of years ago that Jesus would love. The group was ethnically and demographically diverse; some members had kids and some didn't; some were married and some were single. But there was another difference too: there were folks who go to church and those who don't, people who followed Jesus and people who didn't.

The system we have for getting people into small groups does not readily lend itself to this kind of group. Here's how it normally goes: first, you attend church for a while; second, you visit the small groups table and sign up on an interest sheet; third, a small group coordinator places you in a group that fits your schedule; fourth, someone calls you with the time and place of the meeting. The call hopefully comes soon after you sign up, but there could be a wait involved. In fact, sometimes all the small groups are full, so there is a waiting list. It could be a few weeks or months before a spot becomes available.

Think of all those steps! If you had any doubt about whether you *really* wanted to be in a small group, you could chicken out at a few different points. What's more, this structure is biased toward the motivated; it doesn't have a means for gathering those who *aren't* looking to get involved in a small group. In fact, you have to be pretty darn motivated, even once you're in the system.

If you are like me, you have been a part of systems like this (perhaps even creating them!). They're critical for gathering and organizing into small groups those who already want to be in a small group. They are seeking it out and are willing to take initiative to make it happen, even willing to endure the inevitable gliches in systems like this. I call these folks the "pre-motivated." The strongly pre-motivated will get into a small group in spite of wrong phone numbers, bounced back e-mails and poor directions because they are determined. But somehow Bert and Susie—and, as we'll see, Jesus—were able to extend beyond the pre-motivated to invite, welcome and include the "not-yet-motivated." How do you get both the pre-motivated *and* the not-yet-motivated into your small group? How do you gather people who wouldn't come to your church or fellowship meeting in the first place?

JESUS' MODEL

One of the many things I love about Jesus is that he had the amazing ability to draw an incredibly diverse group: devout and sinful, compliant and edgy, women and men, well and sick, powerful and persecuted. It really is remarkable, in the face of present-day challenges to gathering a small group, to contemplate his scope and skill. Somehow Jesus managed to bring people who were open to him in addition to some who were skeptical—and even some who were a little avoidant!

The Gospel of Mark offers a good portrait of Jesus roving about with spiritual eyes, positioning himself to gather more people. After a successful stint in Capernaum teaching crowds and healing many people, Jesus had gained an impressive reputation. People were flocking to him, wanting to be healed. The situation grew so dramatic that "the whole town gathered at the door" (Mark 1:33) of the place where Jesus was healing.

Pause at this point and imagine Jesus' situation. The comfortable place would be where people are "signing up," where they already know Jesus and are pre-motivated to be a part of his ministry. He could have set up shop and had a marvelous healing ministry; the sick in Capernaum would have kept him busy for some time, and undoubtedly people would have traveled from distant places to benefit from his skill. Staying in Capernaum would have been an obvious choice, benefiting so many people who obviously *wanted* his attention.

But that isn't what Jesus does. Instead, he goes away to "a solitary place, where he prayed" (Mark 1:35). The story then develops further, with his friends going to find him and telling him that all the people are looking for him, and what Jesus says next is worthy of our attention: "Let us go somewhere else—to the nearby villages—so I can preach there also. That is why I have come" (Mark 1:38). Jesus resists the idea that he will stay where people seek him; rather he will go, continuing his search and rescue mission, making sure that those who might otherwise slip through the cracks hear his message.

Jesus doesn't shape his ministry like you might expect. I imagine the disciples' surprise as Jesus says that they are moving on. "What!?! Why not stay here with those people who really want your attention?" Jesus implicit reply is "No, we're taking this thing out further and broader than you imagined. *That* is why I came."

The fact that Jesus came out with this definitive plan after a time away, praying, gives me more than a subtle clue about God's heart for people. Jesus goes away to pray during an impressively fruitful time of teaching and healing, and he comes out with direction *toward* those *less* motivated to follow him. I should pay attention to that. How should our small group gathering strategies reflect God's heart for humans and Jesus' example while he lived?

INITIAL GATHERING

We had it all worked out. More than a dozen freshman small group leaders had committed to living in the dorms their sophomore year; a radical decision at University of California–Davis, where protocol was to get out of the noisy, often unair-conditioned dorms as quickly as possible. But these students had caught a vision for doing the kind of ministry they had seen Jesus do. They wanted to seek out relationships with students who might not intentionally seek out relationship with God. They were compelled by the example of Jesus to reach students who were not-yet-motivated.

It was spring, and the students were slated to re-enter the dorms the following fall. Then the campus housing policy changed. Due to heavy enrollment, only freshmen would be allowed to live in the dorms. Sophomores no longer had the option to live among the students that they hoped to gather into their small groups.

Believing that they were not to give up, we did everything we could think of to be in and around the dorms where the small group leaders had intended to live. Sophomores helped freshmen carry boxes on move-in day. They hung out and played Frisbee in the lawns around the dorms. They ate meals in the dining facility. They were vigilant about memorizing names and making note of contact information, following up with a visit, a "dormroom-warming" gift like a plant or a box of tissues, or an invitation to go to Wal-Mart or out for frozen yogurt. They looked for every conceivable opportunity to meet people in those dorms and join in on whatever was happening there.

In the end, every group had a mix of people who had come to ministry events and signed up for a small group, *and* people who had never dreamed of being in a small group in their lives! Gathering a small group took on a whole new meaning; applying Jesus' model to our ministry wasn't limited to living in the dorms. We learned that there is no end to the creativity in applying all that Jesus has taught us about gathering. And even though we thought we had been thwarted, it worked!

Other contexts offer other seemingly insurmountable blocks to gathering beyond the pre-motivated. I have worked with campus ministers whose access to the dorms was severely limited. Dorms can seem about as welcoming as a maximum-security prison, and with good reason. On these campuses, campus ministers and students alike have come up with creative ideas to position themselves for relationships with new students in the first three weeks of school. At University of Maryland, Baltimore County, campus ministers and student leaders attended many of the welcome week events that were for freshmen but open to the larger community. There they prayed for divine contacts. At Johns Hopkins University, campus ministers and student leaders hung out in public spaces, simply availing themselves to students who needed directions or had a little time to talk. They also planned some big dinners at an apartment close to campus that they could invite people to. On the second day students arrived, they hosted a dinner for close to sixty people that they were then able to invite to join small groups.

One Filipino student, Lea, got a vision for gathering a small group specifically for other Filipino students. She went to a part of the student union where many Filipino students gathered to connect and made that place her second home. She also attended secular Filipino club meetings, all the while inviting people to her small group. What developed was a vibrant community of friends, some of whom never would have come to a small group otherwise. At the end of the year, two of the students decided to continue the group and became leaders!

PARTICULARLY CRITICAL TIMES

These examples illustrate another important point about gathering small groups. The students and staff were *positioning themselves* to be available during a *particularly critical time*. The first three weeks at college represent a total overhaul of a student's community and, often, their life's trajectory.

I actually came to college *determined* to change my life's trajectory; I *wanted* to figure out who God was. The day I moved into my freshman dorm Joe and Dave, who were followers of Jesus, helped me assemble my loft bed. Those guys were a part of my initial contact with a community that would help me wrestle through what it meant to follow Jesus.

A colleague of mine says, "The first 10-20 days on campus are critical for (freshman) bonding. After these critical days, the average [freshman] has bonded with 90% of all the significant people she will relate to in the [first] year."[1] What I have seen in ministry over the years has confirmed his insight. People in our fellowships who wound up being best of friends met in the first days of freshman year. My husband's ten-year col-

---

[1]Mark Phifer-Houseman, "Bonding and the Frosh Leader's Task: Incarnation Ministry in InterVarsity," unpublished paper, 1995, p. 4.

lege reunion was organized by freshman dorm groupings, because that was where the most significant friendships had been formed. A critical window of opportunity, then, is the first twenty days of the first year of college. Small group leaders who bond with people in that window of time potentially can become very naturally a part of their lives.

One small group leader took this to heart. Rebekah lived off campus in an apartment, but she committed to being in the freshman dorm where she was leading a small group every single day for the first three weeks of the school year. Her goal was to be "like furniture"; she wanted to make her presence so normal in that dorm that people would see her as a fixture. She visited, hung out, played games, watched movies, popped popcorn—she even went to the dorm dance. After one week, people were calling her an honorary dorm member!

If Rebekah had tried to initiate this in November, she would have had a much harder time. Relationships would have already been established, and peoples' schedules would have already been filled. In fact, I would suggest that it would be difficult, if not impossible, to bond like she did at any other time in the year. She positioned herself during an open window of opportunity that does *not* stay open for long.

Whatever the particular community or campus situation, the principle of gathering can be creatively applied. There are similar windows that exist naturally; small group leaders should ponder them as well:

- The start of the school year is a significant start-up time for many families, who are shifting their schedules in a variety of ways.

- Seasons in the church calendar, like Advent and Lent, can function as windows of opportunity.

- Many people are motivated for something new at the beginning of the calendar year or when they first move to a
  new location. I know that when I moved to Baltimore from
  California, there was a period of time during which we said
  yes to any invitation that came our way! The people who
  would talk to us in the park became our primary social contacts.

If small group leaders can attempt to gather groups during natural windows of opportunity like these, then it will be
much more likely that they will have success reaching the
not-yet-motivated.

No two situations are exactly alike, so applying one strategy to every situation simply won't work. Rather, think
through the following steps to discern what will work best in
your context.

1. Pray for the Father's heart for your campus or church.
   Pray that your attitude toward your campus or church
   would be similar to the Father's: "not wanting anyone to
   perish, but everyone to come to repentance" (2 Peter 3:9).
   In other words, pray that you would seek out not just the
   pre-motivated but especially the not-yet-motivated.

2. Discern what particularly critical times exist for the people
   you hope to gather into small groups.

3. Develop a strategy that allows you to bond with individuals
   during those critical windows of opportunity.

REGATHERING

After practicing these principles at UC–Davis for a number of
years, we noticed a disturbing trend: we were losing people
their sophomore year, and the ones who stayed in the fellow-

ship often felt marginalized and disconnected. I was losing sleep over this! Seeing people I dearly cared about who had been thriving in their freshman year drop out of the fellowship became unacceptable to me.

A lot of factors were at work. The second year at UC–Davis was difficult for students in our fellowship. After being the focus of literally every campus outreach endeavor and living in the relative haven of the dorms, sophomores were made to move off campus. Second-year students moved into often-overcrowded apartments with other students who were struggling through the same transition. This was a particularly critical time for these students, but no one saw it coming. You know you are supposed to experience a significant change your freshman year, but sophomore year? By then you're supposed to have it all together.

After some careful analysis of the situation and a great deal of prayer, we decided that the best way to engage what we had begun to call "sophomore syndrome" was through small groups. Our challenge became *re*gathering students.

In the past, we had formed sophomore and upperclassmen small groups in the fall. Once we identified the sophomore syndrome, we decided to ease the transition by organizing groups for people in the spring of their freshman year. We tried to keep natural groupings of friends in the same groups so that no one felt like they were starting over. Then, before the year ended, each newly formed small group had a social gathering together and exchanged e-mail addresses, so they could have some contact over the summer.

The leaders of these groups, applying lessons learned from our experience reaching out to new students, committed together to visiting the apartment of every group member within the first week of school that fall. Faced with another window of opportunity, they positioned themselves accordingly. Rather than losing touch and falling through the cracks, students came into their second year already grafted into a small group and maintaining relationship with some key friends from the previous year's group. In the end, the process of regathering became nearly as important as the initial gathering in the life of our fellowship. We saw a dramatic increase in the number of sophomores staying in our fellowship and were able to see Jesus continue his process of working in them!

Every Christian community and campus has its own unique set of challenges and opportunities. For UC–Davis it was sophomore syndrome; at your school it could be senior syndrome. In my church, I have seen the need for regathering at different transition points of life: when people move from college to career age; when people have children; when children get busy with consuming activities; when people return to graduate school or change jobs. The need for regathering exists in most contexts, and similar principles apply. Regathering can help us follow Jesus' call to persist in loving people for the long haul.

For me, addressing the regathering issue has meant being creative: sometimes meeting in the morning or on weekends; sometimes scheduling shorter or less frequent meetings; sometimes building a meal into the group experience. One small group I was in had a lot of families with young children. We observed drop-off happening as babysitters canceled unexpectedly or the cost of hiring them became prohibitive. We decided to meet at church so that we could hire one babysitter for all the children and use the Sunday school room, which was stocked with toys.

No one plan will suit every context. Careful thought and prayer needs to be given to the particulars in your situation.

1. Recognize the transitions that people are going through in your fellowship or community.

2. Gauge the relative impact of these transition on drop-off.

3. Strategize about what would help to ease each transition.

4. Develop a small group structure that will serve individuals as they move *into and through* the transition.

GATHERING THE PRE-MOTIVATED

As we broaden our small group gathering process to reach the not-yet-motivated, we still need to have systems in place to support the pre-motivated. Even highly pre-motivated people will give up if the process is arduous or takes too long.

In the campus situation, without a clear strategy for quick follow up, weeks can pass before the first small group meeting takes place. This misses the three-week window of opportunity to bond with new students at the most natural time of the year. To make the most of a window of opportunity, the turn-around needs to be much faster, with initial follow-up happening within twenty-four hours of a person indicating interest. On one of the campuses in our area, leaders realized that their strategy was not working well enough. They had sign-up cards at their welcome week events, and they offered new students the ability to choose open spaces for small group based on their schedules, hobbies, interests and even topics. But the process of analyzing the data and grouping people according to all of these factors was so difficult that small groups didn't start meeting until after the third week of school, well after many new students had filled their calendars with other commitments and relationships.

The students rethought their strategy with speed in mind. They decided to ask only for information that was absolutely *essential* on the initial sign-up card: name, age, gender, dorm, e-mail, phone, etc. With that information in hand, a small group leader would follow up within twenty-four hours. Personal relationships started *while* the leaders figured out the when and where of the small group meeting, rather than the other way around.

Another group of students tried something new at the first large group meeting of the year. As a part of the content of the meeting, their small group structure was explained. Some of the small groups were geographic (dorm-based or in certain apartment complexes), but some were forming around majors, affinity groups or interests. The people in attendance divided into those groupings and met their prospective small group leaders. Several of the groupings did something together after the meeting—grabbing ice cream or hanging out back at the dorm.

Alex Kirk devised a wonderful plan for gathering the pre-motivated into his campus fellowship. During the summer, many of his current students worshiped with pre-motivated incoming freshmen. He sent his students home for the summer with invitations to sign up in advance for the initial Inter-Varsity gatherings. This process made making contact with those folks easy, and was a wonderful welcome for the new students as well.

GATHERING IN THE E-WORLD

Can you believe there was a time when small group leaders had to coordinate events by making phone calls from a land-line? That meant small group leaders were stuck to a wall, hoping that the recipient of their call was stuck to their own wall. How did they do it?

In many respects, gathering a small group is made much easier with the Internet. At McDaniel College, a small group leader named Christie began welcoming incoming freshmen that had joined the "McDaniel" Facebook group the summer before they set foot on campus. Christie was able to help connect people who were living in the same area for a small group. When the students came to school, they already had a relational start with their small group leader and other freshmen that would be in their group! They had a sense of belonging before even meeting in the flesh. As much as we can utilize this medium for the sake of gathering small groups, fantastic!

Overall, our means of connecting with people on the computer is a blessing and absolutely should be a part of our strategy to gather small groups. We would be crazy not to take advantage of the ease of it, how comfortable people are with it as a medium, and how convenient it is to disseminate details like time and location quickly. However, we should not be tempted to believe that this *means* to developing community is all we need.

Consider the number of communications most people receive in one day. The Internet can function like one of those posting places on campus with seventy-five fliers announcing events on campus. Too much information at once, and the messages blend together. In a world where people have eight hundred Facebook friends, being one of them doesn't make you part of their community. Don't be fooled into thinking that your message will necessarily stand out. What *will* stand out is your personal openness to a real friendship.

THE COST AND BLESSING INVOLVED IN GATHERING

The most profound comfort I have when counting the cost of gathering a small group is the fact that Jesus did it. It could have all happened another way, but it didn't. Jesus came and lived a relational life among human beings in order to gather people into God's family. It wasn't easy, but it is the life he chose, out of love, and the life he invites us into as small group leaders and gatherers. The people who will be in our small groups are people that Jesus loves.

Effective gathering of the pre-motivated and not-yet-motivated, and regathering after particularly critical times, require more commitment than perhaps we expect is involved in leading a small group. At UC–Davis, small group leaders would wrestle through what the commitment would look like for their first three weeks of school. Those conversations were not without tears as students committed to being a daily presence in the dorms or apartments, or attending affinity group meetings at every opportunity. Before the start of the outreach effort, many of the leaders would talk with family or roommates to explain their temporary absence while they made the effort to gather during this particular window of opportunity. The leaders would ask their friends for their blessing and grace while they did the ministry of gathering. Sometimes, their friends would become their prayer partners, commissioning them into the dorms or out into other apartments. I even heard of one friend who offered to do their chores for them during the intensive time of gathering.

The gathering process can also be emotionally difficult on a personal level. It requires a certain fortitude to knock on a virtual stranger's door, and we all risk rejection when we initiate friendship. Frankly, it's easier to stay at home. I felt awkward, at age twenty-six, hanging out in a freshman dorm. During the beginning of one year, every time I visited a freshman named Heather, the first thing she would say was "What are you doing here?" I could only hope that the tension inside me that her curt greeting raised didn't show when I answered casually, "Just here to see how it's going!"

Heather wound up being a core member of my small group, and her life was changed by Jesus that year. We also ended up being friends. I am so grateful that I had been challenged to press through my own insecurities so that I could reach out to her. Otherwise, I cannot imagine how she would have gotten into a small group, and I would not have had my own faith challenged as I saw her life transformed.

Jesus lived his life, even the suffering of the cross, "for the joy set before him" (Hebrews 12:2). We can expect to receive the same joy as Jesus as we follow in the steps of his life. The sacrifice will, in the end, be counted as gain as we see people who might never have considered the gospel gathered into God's family. And there is blessing for each of us as we expand our own circles of friendship to include more people that Jesus loves. My prayer is that you will trust in the joy that is set before you as you go forward in gathering people together into these critical forums for ministry.

3

SMALL GROUPS AS COMMUNITY

Sandra Van Opstal

A CHRISTIAN I KNOW recently told me that he doesn't need to go to church to live out his faith in Jesus. He reads Scripture, prays, sees a spiritual mentor and actively engages in mission, but he does not need to be involved regularly with other believers. I was sad for him because he was missing out on a meaningful group experience, but I also needed to correct him: Jesus does not only call us to himself; he calls us to be a part of a community.

Community has become popular in this faith generation; I think there is an unspoken rule that it has to be in every organization's mission statement. But it's not at all clear from organization to organization, from person to person, what we expect to see when that mission is accomplished. What exactly do we mean by *community*?

WHY DO WE GET TOGETHER?

The word *community* has its roots in Latin and means "common, public, shared by all or many." A *community* is a unified group of people who share common circumstances, beliefs and values, and who look for ways to embrace (or work through) their differences. But we breathe the air of individualism. Modern society values independence above almost anything else. When I was a corporate trainer at a Fortune 500 company, I actually taught associates in the company to think in terms of WIIFM (What's in it for me?). In doing so, I contributed to this idea that life is *for* each individual, in opposition to being for one another. Community becomes a means to an end—more about what we can gain from one another than what we contribute to our collective experience. Such a distorted perspective demands a more compelling vision of true community.

A Christian community is a community because it is unified, though not primarily by circumstance or even by values or beliefs. A Christian community, as the apostle Paul suggests, is unified by our common life in Christ.

> You are no longer foreigners and aliens, but fellow citizens with God's people and members of God's household, built on the foundation of the apostles and prophets, with Christ Jesus himself as the chief cornerstone. In him the whole building is joined together and rises to become a holy temple in the Lord. And in him you too are being built together to become a dwelling in which God lives by his Spirit. (Ephesians 2:19-22)

Paul uses collective language, giving the Ephesian church a picture of a beautiful building with Christ as the cornerstone—the most important weight-bearing stone in the building. This vision is vivid and exciting: we can imagine what we are becoming. We are together being built together as a people in which God's Spirit can dwell.

Have you ever envisioned your small group in this way? Small groups on college campuses and in churches are meeting in dorms or homes and becoming small palaces for the king of the universe as they are united by a common call to follow Christ.

I was introduced to small group community by accident. As a student at a small liberal arts school in the Midwest, I headed out to work out one day and stumbled across an InterVarsity small group. A friend asked me if I wanted to stay. It was the last thing I wanted to do at the time; although I was a Christian, I thought of such groups as something like broccoli—good for you but not particularly good. I had been operating under the unconscious assumption that a building could be built with just two bricks: Jesus and me.

But for some reason, when my friend asked me to stay, I said yes. Through that small group experience I realized that a Christian small group—a community that studies the Bible, prays and participates in God's mission together for the purposes of God's transforming work—is a gift from God.

WHY ARE WE TOGETHER?

It is not enough, of course, to meet together and say, "Hey, we are a community because Jesus brings us together. Look at us!" Christians in community are meant to guide one another in the process of transformation, through the love and the grace of Christ, to become and behave more like Jesus. In community we have the exciting opportunity and responsibility to do life together.

Jenny was distressed and wanted to meet "right away." As she sat down to explain the problems her small group was having, I held my breath. Who knew what it could be?

"Well" she began, "Our small group is too big." *What a problem!* I thought. Jenny was leading a small group in a dorm that she did not live in. There was no Christian presence established there, and by mid-semester the small group of six freshmen she had hoped for had grown to twenty highly invested people. She had never expected the group to be so big. What had happened?

Group ownership had happened. Small groups are not "mine," they're "ours." At least they should be.

You know you've developed group ownership when members begin to refer to the group as "ours." Although there are many ways to develop ownership for a community, a few general categories have proven effective.

1. *Establish a group identity.* Involve participants in choosing which passages of Scripture to study, setting ground rules for the community or deciding whether to be open to new members or visitors, or closed in order to establish a safe environment for greater vulnerability and intimacy in conversation.

2. *Ensure that people's passions and gifts are being utilized.* In a group with high ownership, members will be encouraged to share the things they are excited about doing with the group. This may include leading worship, coordinating outings, sending e-mails and modeling evangelism.

3. *Create shared experiences.* When I was growing up, my best friend's mom regularly told us that we were "makin' memories" together. Shared experiences—taking place both during group meetings and informally outside scheduled meetings—reinforces and deepens ownership. This happens as we socialize together, as we collaborate on

serving projects and as we help each other with significant tasks. Our small group, for example, comes together to help every time someone moves into a new home.

WHY DO WE STAY TOGETHER?

A thing to keep in mind, however, is that different backgrounds—gender, culture, ethnicity—affect how we approach forming community and how we "feel" community. We had a small group for freshmen once called "Bagels, Bibles and Blab." It was successful in part because sitting around, talking and eating together can make great memories for a group of women. I am not sure the same approach would have worked for the men in our fellowship.

Not only do the ways communities form differ, but a group's ongoing activities may not "feel" like a community-forming experience for everyone. One small group I started during the summer lived together, served together in the neighborhood and studied Scripture together daily for weeks. One of the members complained about how we were not a community. "Community is really lacking," he said. "We really need to work on it."

I was confused! We had overcome some very difficult situations, such that I felt I knew these people better than some of my best friends at home. As he explained what was going on for him, I began to realize what he was missing: his idea of "community" was lots of socializing, through games and the like. He was right; we had not played any games. But what did games have to do with community?

It turns out he had grown up playing games and talking trash as a means of building a common bond in his church. This was not the church culture I had grown up in; I had to have him teach me. We incorporated some intentional "fun" here and there, and he felt much better about our community. I was glad I asked!

WHAT DO WE OFFER EACH OTHER?

"If you do not mind me asking, how much do you spend on food per month?" This is a recent e-mail I sent to a couple in our small group. Our group is made up of people from a variety of backgrounds learning to seek God's transformation in finances, mission and justice. That means we study God's Word and seek to respond in action that is consistent with belief. The average American family of two spends an excessive amount per month on food; my husband and I are way below the national average, but we noticed that this other couple was spending even less, out of their own commitment to simple living. "So, what do you spend? We want to have people over and provide hospitality, but we are spending more then we want to. We need help."

Building community leads to greater honesty and mutual accountability, which in turn reinforces community. I have been a part of small groups whose view of accountability has been "telling on yourself to other people." However, the Scriptures show us that accountability is more proactive than that. It's not just talking about what *has* happened but what *could* happen. It's not only about where you have been but where you want to be. Accountability is a catalyst for transformation through *encouragement, challenge* and *confession.*

Encouragement. Hebrews 10:24 lets us know that we should "consider how we may spur one another on toward love and good deeds." Interestingly enough, most small group members see the importance of and enjoy encouraging, but few are willing to receive encouragement. One woman I talked

with was really struggling in her first year as an inner-city
school teacher. I asked her why she had not told anyone in her
small group. "I feel like I will burden people with my job, and
even though I am sure I was walking through depression I just
didn't want to bring others into it." I reminded her that the
people in her community would love to listen and pray, and
that others in her group had gone through similar struggles.
Small groups should be communities in which we are willing
not only to encourage but to be encouraged by others.

Challenge. It's not always fun to give or receive, but God
uses people to challenge us. Proverbs 27:17 says, "As iron
sharpens iron, so one man sharpens another." Small groups
ought to be metal shops where we are molded and sharpened
by one another. But who wants that!? On a recent birthday, I
unwrapped a gift excited about what I would find. My friend
Jessica has a knack for getting me gifts and sending me cards
that are full of messages—encouragements, challenges or re-
bukes. This gift, it turns out, was a frame with the words "It's
all about me" engraved in it. Inside that frame was my picture
and the verse "God opposes the proud but gives grace to the
humble" (James 4:6; 1 Peter 5:5; cf. Proverbs 3:34). I didn't
know whether to laugh or cry—to feel loved or offended or
both. True to form, though, with this gift Jessica was saying
she loved me and wanted me to keep becoming more like
Jesus. The people that are committed to us show it by not
leaving us where we are; they love us by encouraging, challenging and correcting us.

Confession. Sharing our sin with each other is hard. We fear
judgment and rejection, but God designed us to experience
grace and acceptance from our brothers and sisters! While
confessing to God brings me forgiveness, confessing to our
community brings healing. Without confession our sin pulls us

into isolation. Sin is afraid of the light, and confession brings it out of the darkness and helps to make sin powerless over us.

The culture that people grew up in can greatly impact their desire and ability to engage in this kind of accountability. Some people may be uncomfortable with sharing vulnerably with a whole group—this may be especially true of a group that includes both men and women. Such people may be more comfortable pairing off with a prayer partner to pursue mutual accountability. Some people may be used to high levels of vulnerability by church leaders and members, while others may not be. When I first worked with Asian American students, I talked candidly about areas of rebellion that God has helped me to overcome. They were shocked; many of them weren't used to leaders confessing such things. Another small group was, with the exception of myself and one other person, made up of white people. When we left, the African American woman expressed that she had been unwilling to be candid until she reached a certain level of trust with the other group members. I have been in conversations with people who are open to the "opinions" and "thoughts" of others, but the idea of submission to a community is countercultural to them. Creating an environment where people are willing to encourage, challenge and confess in light of such differences may take some thinking.

When John said, "I am gay," my mouth dropped to the floor, not because of what he said but because he actually shared it with the group. We had been meeting with twenty-five freshmen on campus for discipleship. I actually have no recollection of the topic of discussion that day. The only thing I remember is that John shared very vulnerably about what it was like for him to struggle with his sexuality. He wanted God to restore him, but he had no community to help him. As an African American man, he had endured a double stigma against questioning his sexual identity, hearing nothing but jokes on the street and condemnation in the church about "those gays." Our group was the first place he felt safe enough to confess his brokenness. His community became a source of healing not only for him but for others as well.

WHAT DO WE COMMIT TO EACH OTHER?

Sofia's small group heard during prayer time that her computer had broken down and that she was not able to purchase a new one. Jen wasn't sure she wanted to let on that she did not come from a wealthy family, since most of the other students had parents who were executives in major corporations. She felt ashamed, but she also felt stressed out; she really needed prayer. Her small group surrounded her and prayed for God to provide. Then they did what many do not do: they actually became the answer to their prayers for Sofia.

"We can raise this money for her!" one member said. "Let's send an e-mail out to our friends and family and larger fellowship, and ask if anyone wants to be a part of buying a new computer." Another member spoke up: "Well, she is very private about her situation, so let's not say who it is for. We don't want to take away her dignity." Within a week the group collected enough money to purchase a computer for Sofia. Some used their technical skills to build it and install all the software, others used their networking to send out e-mails and connect with people about the situation. Everyone pitched in so that by Friday she had a working computer on her dorm desk. It was the most tangible expression of love I had ever seen by a small group.

Such acts of kindness seem simple enough, but sometimes we need to be reminded that people's needs are not only spiritual but also emotional and physical. Communities that find tangible ways of serving one another stand out! What might your small group do tangibly for one another?

1. *Share your stuff.* Whether it is sharing textbooks with someone who doesn't have the money to buy them, or a grill for someone who wants to have a backyard barbecue, we are likely to have members in our small group that do not always have access to the wealth that others have. We are also likely to have, somewhere among the resources of our group, access to the particular needs of a group member at any given moment.

2. *Share your gifts.* We have unique gifts and talents to offer one another. This year we have had a member of our small group who was struggling to find a job. My husband, who has conducted many interviews, offered to do some mock interviews with him to prepare him for his search. The Hezekiah Walker song "I Need You to Survive" is a helpful reminder that we are called the body of Christ for a reason: each expression of Christ's body has in itself what's needed for the whole body to flourish; we should not withhold ourselves from each other. Community is not just nice; it's necessary!

WHAT ABOUT OUR DIFFERENCES?

Recently I was at a Christian university training resident assistants. We were discussing the need to be meaningfully involved with people who are different from us.[1] I walked over to a table of students and asked them what they were discussing. "Honestly," they confessed, "the idea that we need

---

[1]For a good discussion of this need for diversity, see Brenda Salter McNeil, *A Credible Witness* (Downers Grove, Ill.: InterVarsity Press, 2008).

people who are different is just foreign to us. We're not used to thinking that way." I was floored. Here were the student leaders of a Christian institution that produces church leaders, and they didn't understand a very real need.

Although we are united by Christ to one another, we are all not the same. Christians come from different backgrounds, life experiences and ethnicities. This ensures that we will never be bored!

One of the ways differences in background, preferences and ethnicity can bring growth and stimulation to our walk with God is in the discipline of prayer. Our background and experience impacts how we pray: some have learned to pray in groups liturgically; others, out loud one at a time; still others, out loud, all at the same time. Our background and experience also impacts the content of our prayers. When I joined the gospel choir on our campus I realized that many of these students prayed about things my wealthier students did not pray about, prayers like "God, you are the great provider, and I pray that my check comes in so I can buy books." My perspective of the struggles of life and my understanding of God's power increased. God was a provider in a way those of us who were financially well off just didn't seem to notice!

Our praise, worship and celebration of God are also impacted heavily by the communities that we come from. Each community tends to emphasize a particular aspect of God's character to celebrate.[2] Songs with certain flavors and themes remind us of the God we know and how we prefer to interact with him. When we come together in community with people who are different from us, our style of worship and our understanding of God can be expanded.

---

[2]For an excellent book on this, check out Gordon Chandler, *God's Global Mosaic* (Downers Grove, Ill.: InterVarsity Press, 2000).

Latino worship is extremely celebratory and communal. It involves the whole body and the whole "body." We love to celebrate how God has been at work in our lives and in the lives of the community as a weekly, if not daily, activity. Thinking it was just "normal" to do this, I began to open up leadership meetings in our campus fellowship with a time of celebration. We met monthly, so I wanted to catch up with how God had been at work in the life of each leader. I made an invitation: *silence.*

We did this for months, then years. I taught on celebration and read psalms to the group, and yet it still felt like I was pulling teeth. But after four years we had a community that regularly celebrated God's goodness together. Many students expressed to me that this Latino tradition of celebration was a gift to them. They needed me!

Our understanding of God is likewise expanded as we study the Scriptures with people who are different from us. Some of us were taught in church to look for certain things about God as we read the Scriptures. We come in with something in mind already, and it affects *how* we read and even *what* we read. Some communities, for example, love Paul's epistles but have never read or even heard preaching from the Old Testament prophets. One summer at a small group that was meeting as part of an urban project, I asked students to read Psalm 139 from the perspective of the community they had moved into for the summer. They were surprised by the impact of the exercise; after the exercise one woman remarked, "You mean race and ethnicity do affect our view of Scripture?"

When my husband and I bought a house we had one goal in mind: *Get a good house.* The problem was that we had different perspectives. I wanted a large living room (for hosting social gatherings). He was looking at lot size (for a garden) and plumbing (for strong water pressure). Every house I liked he hated, and every house he wanted I wanted to leave. Finally we realized what constituted "a good house" for each of us. Enlightened by our differences, we quickly found a house that helped us live out the convictions we each brought to our marriage. Differences, properly explored and honored, can bring growth and stimulation in our walk with the Lord.

We fear what we don't understand, however, and we run from what we fear. Ethnically diverse small group communities are uncommon because most neighborhoods, churches and campus fellowships are not ethnically diverse. After five years of being in the same small group of campus ministers, one of our members decided to go back to school. "Sandra," she said, "I am so glad that I have had the opportunity to be your friend. Being your friend has helped me to see that what my parents taught me and what I embraced from them about Latinos was wrong. I am so blessed to have grown past my stereotypes of Latinos because of you." *OK,* I was thinking, *should I be offended or blessed or both?* I decided I was blessed: my friend had been "forced" to be in community with me because of our work relationship, but over time God had revealed to her the prejudice she had against my community, and she was able to overcome it. I have had similar experiences as God has called me into community with people I would not otherwise have sought out. I learned not to run from what I fear but to learn from it.

If you are prepared to accept and embrace and even seek out diversity in your small group as a blessing and not a burden, your small group will too. There are three main ways you can do this.

1. *Be willing and open.* It's important for you to identify your own biases. Intentionally building relationships with people who are different will surface and challenge those biases. Reading books or listening to sermons by people from a diversity of backgrounds will help you be willingly open to others.

2. *Foster openness in the group.* You can prepare people in advance to embrace differences in a group. Model by communicating what you have learned from people who are different from you. Use prayers, quotes or songs that come from the experiences of others. Watch movies or attend events that give you a clue into the lives of other communities on your campus or in your church.

3. *Affirm minorities in your group.* It is likely that people in your group who are outnumbered will feel it. Whether it is an Asian American student in a white community, a man in a group of women or a single person in a group full of couples, work hard to include them. It may be good to check in with these members to see how they feel as a part of the group and what you can do to create a better environment.

Members of a Christian community are united by Christ to one another, beyond our differences. We grow with one another in our faith journey. We walk alongside one another through the good, the bad and the ugly. And we have the incredible opportunity to have our understanding of God expanded. What more could we ask for? God has set it up for our *good.*

4

DYNAMICS OF COMMUNITY

Sandra Van Opstal

ONE SUMMER I had the privilege of going to China to teach English. I loved everything about it—the food, the people, the history—but after eating all the delicious mangos my stomach could take and all the melon-flavored popsicles I could consume, I recognized a craving that could have only one solution: chocolate.

I happened upon a man selling popsicles. I didn't know enough Mandarin to ask for chocolate, so I examined the wrapper, pointed at something and asked him, "Chocolate?" He nodded in reassurance. I flung the wrapper off, jammed it in my mouth and took a huge bite . . . only to savor my first red bean popsicle!

Whether it's red bean in China or candies covered with chili pepper in Mexico, I am sure there have been times where you examined the wrapper and assumed something that just wasn't the case. This can happen with our experiences in community as well: sometimes they look like something they are not.

Everyone wanted to be a part of Ryan's small group because it was so cool and diverse. They even took road trips together. They clearly had become a tight-knit group fast! Looking deeper, however, it became clear that they got along so well because they had hardly disagreed on anything substantial and never confronted the areas of one another's lives that needed to change. And although they had a great time, they were never held accountable to the things they studied. All in all, there was very little real transformation: Ana kept partying, Brad's secret sins stayed secret, Migdalia didn't learned to budget her money, and Marcus stayed confused about the grace of God. They had never gone through the process of becoming true community.

STAGES OF COMMUNITY

You may be tempted to compare your small group to other well-functioning ones that you have been in or are aware of. Similarly, it's easy to settle for a community that seems to be well-functioning even if it's really not. In his book *The Different Drum* Scott Peck sees three necessary stages that any community—including your small group—goes through before arriving at *true community*.[1]

When small group members are just getting to know one another, everyone is looking for common ground. They often gloss over differences. Peck calls this stage *pseudocommunity.* Jan's small group was in this stage: they were close-knit as long as they maintained acceptable norms. During this stage the focus of conversation will be shared experiences and values. Participating in ice breakers, sharing life stories and setting ground rules are a part of this stage. Once the

---

[1]See M. Scott Peck, *The Different Drum* (New York: Simon & Schuster, 1987).

individual members of the group get a sense of who the others are, they build trust based on those commonalities and continue to grow as they learn from Scripture and enjoy one another's company. It feels great!

Often small groups will stay in this stage for long periods because it feels comfortable. They enjoy the harmony of this stage, but its foundation is weak. Pseudocommunity is an excellent place to start but a bad place to settle.

When a group realizes that they can't ignore all of their differences, they enter into the stage of *chaos*. They begin to give voice to disagreements and differences. Members may begin to verbalize different theological perspectives or interpretations of a text. Sometimes the disagreement causes the chaos, and sometimes the way they communicate the disagreement is the culprit. It seems as if the group is growing apart.

Don't lose heart, because this is actually a good sign. In conversation with one of Jan's group members, I realized that there were people that really wanted to discuss their differences. Part of the group's appeal had been its diversity; people had hoped to learn from those who were different from them. After years with Jan's group, this person decided to join another group that "fought well"—like a family. In her first time at Ernesto's small group, people shared deeply and disagreed passionately. It was clear that they had done this before and as the leader Ernesto asked questions to probe into their different perspectives. It was both uncomfortable and refreshing. This group was not in chaos; they had established a set of norms that included their differences.

If you've ever been a part of a group in chaos you know that it's uncomfortable; for some, it is almost unbearable. Believers are united beyond our differences, but that does not mean that differences do not create tension. The ability of the small group leader to help a group navigate differences is critical. We will address this in more depth in the section on conflict, but while learning to navigate conflict is important for the growth of the group, there are some differences that can't be resolved, and not everyone can get their way all the time. Each member needs to unlearn the factors that keep them from building true community.

The *emptiness* stage requires that individuals die to certain beliefs or behaviors. The model for this stage is Christ, who emptied himself. As Christians, at the cross we are called to a lifestyle of this counterintuitive but fundamental emptying, putting others' needs above our own.

Wayne's small group was full of folks from diverse denominational backgrounds, which made for lively conversation. A particular group member was regularly making dogmatic, anti-Catholic remarks. Eventually the Catholic group members left, leading the group to an experience of emptiness.

This group member, we determined, was driven in part by an inflated ego. Individual members need guidance through chaos to recognize their need for repentance and new behaviors. As they empty themselves of their individual prejudices, the group as a whole can come to a place of consensus. If the members are not willing to empty themselves, the group will continue to experience dissonance, chaos and ultimately death. But even this death can pave the way for the birth of a new creature: the *true community*.

The mark of a community that has moved through its chaos is a deep understanding of one another. They come to understand that there are bound to be differences with one another. Meanwhile, they've built trust together as individual members emptied themselves of prejudices or behaviors—whether these were mere clashes of temperament or deeper, sinful tendencies—that were causing pain for other members. Dis-agreements no longer lead people to question one another's intentions. A foundation of trust allows for even heated discussions and lively confrontation.

Small groups that have achieved true community are some of the most fulfilling places to be. They have persisted through challenges of comfortable superficiality, through clashes of perspective, through experiences of loss and disappointment, to an environment of mutual understanding and common concern. (See figure 4.1.) Members not only celebrate together and have fun, but they deeply understand one another and have learned to be a part of each other's process of transformation.

Figure 4.1. The progression of true community

The small group leader is a necessary guide from one stage to the next, as true community inevitably entails conflict.

CONFLICT IN COMMUNITY

In the context of community, conflict is not necessarily bad; it usually involves relational tension between people due to differing views and values. No one likes tension—some may want to run from it—but leaders embrace tension as a way to resolution. Indeed, God takes joy in using us in his ministry of reconciliation.

When I first arrived at Northwestern University as the InterVarsity staff worker, the student team I worked with was hurting. One of the areas of concern for me was the lack of community. I might not have been so alarmed if it wasn't the small group coordinators with the problem. These were the people that were supposed to model healthy community and conflict, but they did not seem to know how vital this was to their jobs.

As I began to lead the small group coordinators through their disagreements, it became clear that many of them did not have good models for conflict in their homes, churches or friendships. No one had ever taught them to fight well! In order to guide us toward *true community*, I had to walk them through some training in conflict.

Many folks have little firsthand experience of the forgiveness, compassion and humility that ought to mark conflicts among followers of Christ. Conflict resolution is a skill that leaders of communities *must* develop, model and teach. Some of the conflicts that you participate in will be between individuals, and some will be in a small group setting. Peacemaker Ministries offers some suggestions for navigating conflict as it happens.[2]

1. *Take a minute!* If you enter conflict without preparing emotionally, you may slip into careless responses. Sometimes even unrelated circumstances can prevent a person from engaging conflict on a healthy level. It is wise to "hit pause," to wait until the gut feelings associated with the conflict subside. It may take a few seconds, minutes or hours.

2. *Affirm the relationships in conflict.* The best conflict is had when there is a foundation of trust to rely on. The more

---

[2]Adapted from Peacemakers Group Study, accessible at <www.peacemaker.net>.

trust, the easier it is to communicate honestly. Spend some time affirming the commitment to one another and laying ground rules.

3. *Seek understanding.* It will benefit the relationship and the conflict if all the people involved are seeking to understand one another's interests and perspectives.

4. *Evaluate and create solutions.* Reconciliation requires repentance (true change) from wrongdoing and forgiveness of the wrongdoer. One goal of conflict should be a common understanding of what happened and practical steps to avoid repeating mistakes.

Small group leaders need to understand our default style of conflict and to be able to adapt our style depending on the situation, or else we run the risk of creating more tension. Our approach is shaped by our temperment, experience and background. The same is true of other people in any given conflict. The Thomas-Kilmann Conflict Mode Instrument identifies five approaches to conflict, one of which will dominate for each person.[3]

1. The *competing* style is typically assertive and uncooperative. An individual defends a position as an issue of right and wrong. They will not compromise on something of importance, but they can find it hard to value differences and can neglect the importance of relationship.

2. The *accommodating* style is unassertive and cooperative. The individual smoothes over differences and is often called

---

[3]Kenneth W. Thomas and Ralph H. Kilmann, *Thomas-Kilmann Conflict Mode Instrument* (Mountain View, Calif.: CPP, 1974), accessed May 29, 2009, at <www kilmann.com/conflict.html>.

yielding. They see most things as negotiable and rarely see things as worth fighting for. They may give up personal goals and values, but they tend to preserve relationships.

3. The *avoiding* style is unassertive and uncooperative. The individual sees conflicts as necessarily causing broken relationships and pain, and so avoids dealing with it. While diplomatically postponing an issue until a better time is sometimes appropriate, avoiding conflict leaves both the individual's goals and the relationship vulnerable.

4. The *compromising* style is moderately assertive and cooperative. The individual believes everyone should give a little and lose a little. It is somewhere between competing and accommodating, and it faces the issue directly rather than avoiding. The downfall is that both parties might be afraid to have to give up something that is important, so it endangers the relationship. The upside is that it works in situations when time is a factor.

5. The *collaborating* style is assertive and cooperative. The individual's goal is to understand the perspective of the other person and come up with creative solutions to the conflict. This style places a high priority on both the relationship and the goal. This mode is the one that forms the basis for the steps of managing conflict.

While collaboration is an excellent way of managing conflict *directly,* there are other equally biblical, culturally influenced approaches to conflict resolution. Cultural differences can cause tension in a small group, but not taking cultural differences into account *during* conflict resolution may increase the actual tension. Individuals in your community may be operating under a different set of rules for conflict.

In his book *Cross-Cultural Conflict,* Duane Elmer identifies three common problems that arise: (1) each party to a conflict thinks theirs is the "right" way (or even more dangerous, the "biblical" way); (2) people are unaware of the rules that they are using in conflict; (3) the set of rules being used are based on an intricate set of deeply held values and are therefore more complex then either party realizes.[4]

The mind naturally seeks to understand conflict situations, even minor ones. When facts are not immediately forthcoming to explain the ambiguous situations, the mind tends to fill in the blanks. That is, we supply our own data to explain the situation. The fatal flaw is that we provide the understanding from our cultural frame of reference, not from the cultural frame of reference of the other person. . . . The interpretation we provide virtually always attributes a negative characteristic and motivation to the other person. We rarely give people the benefit of the doubt when they do something we do not understand.[5]

There are many non-Western approaches that can aid in this kind of conflict, but one that has proved most helpful to me is the use of a mediator, a third person who acts as an objective party, sorting through miscommunication and difference. The mediator may either have conversations on behalf of a party or sit with both parties present. One mediator helped me to understand a conflict I had with a friend. My friend was waiting to hear me admit fault; I felt I had repeatedly done so. At the end of our conversation, my friend ex-

---

[4]Duane Elmer, *Cross-Cultural Conflict* (Downers Grove, Ill.: InterVarsity Press, 1993), pp. 22-23.
[5]Ibid., p. 18.

pressed a desire to hear me take responsibility for my actions; the mediator said that I already had but that it was getting lost in all of the words I was putting around it. Basically, I was not concise and my friend was missing my point. The conflict might have gone on forever if not for this observation (along with many others) by the mediator.

Small groups are a dynamic and exciting community where people from different backgrounds can edify each other toward God's glory. Part of that means learning to move constructively through conflict and tension together. You can do that through a variety of ways, including

1. Leading a biblical study on a passage that reflects the *attitude* Christians ought to take in conflict: John 4:7-26; 1 Corinthians 1:2-9, 13:7; Matthew 18:12-35.

2. Facilitating a discussion about conflicts group members have had in the past. Group members might recall people who modeled grace at a hard time in life, how that helped and how the group might imitate that person in future conflicts.

3. Exploring the different ways group members' families or culture handle conflict and what the group might learn from one another's experiences.

4. Preparing a conflict case study—sharing a personal story and asking for advice and input on how to handle the situation. (This scenario should involve someone group members don't know.) A more indirect way might be to share a story that contains a lesson within it—like a parable.

Developing an environment where true community can flourish necessarily entails moving as a group through stages of pseudocommunity, chaos and emptiness. Members, including the group leader, will encounter differences, but by approaching the tension that arises intentionally your group can navigate the conflict and build unity. In this process God can display his glory and your group will not only edify its members but be a witness to those on the outside. True community takes time, though, so allow the Holy Spirit to guide you each step of the way, and don't lose heart!

5

NOT *JUST* BIBLE STUDY
THE POWER OF GOD'S WORD IN SMALL GROUPS

Myron Crockett

"WHAT DO YOU THINK of Christians dating non-Christians?"

This was the question Rebecca put before our small group. While discussing how we would live out all the cool things we'd discovered in Genesis 2, the conversation turned to sex and dating. And who could blame these mostly-single grad students? You've just looked at a passage describing the first-ever God-ordained hook-up; a man and a woman are "naked and not ashamed." If you can't have an honest discussion about sex and dating in response to this passage, then you can't do it at all!

Rebecca's question conjured up quizzical looks and thoughtful silence among the group members. "Christians can't date non-Christians," I replied flatly. I was a third-year InterVarsity staff-worker, and I was about as subtle as eight-alarm chili. "Christians relate to non-Christians on Jesus' terms. This involves friendship, love, mutual truth-telling and a

ton of other things. But all these things are done *on Jesus'
terms.* If a Christian and a non-Christian are in a romantic relationship, the Christian's faith-walk with Jesus will always ca-
ter to this relationship. That can't happen if Jesus is Lord."

One of the chapter leaders later revealed to me that Rebecca had been dating a non-Christian for some time. Immediately I began thinking of all the gentler ways I could have
handled her question, all the questions I could have asked her
to find out more about where she was coming from. I had
even more time to ponder this when Rebecca didn't show up
to small group for the next few weeks. She had been a very
devoted member of our group. One thought did laps in my
head like a gerbil on a wheel: *Good job, doofus!*

Doofus small group leader or not, Rebecca returned to our
group after a few weeks. She participated fully, and it was like
nothing had happened—that is, until after the study. Rebecca
came up to me and said, "Sorry I haven't been around for a
few weeks. I had a lot of work to do in class, and I had to study
like crazy. Oh, and I just wanted you to know that I broke up
with my boyfriend."

This was an occasion for bad news and fantastic news. The
bad news: *I was still a tactless doofus.* The fantastic (and far
more important than my dooficity) news: *Rebecca had made
a significant heart-change for Jesus in response to God's
Word!* A Bible study on Genesis 2 had been an open door to
spiritual maturity for a Christian sister.

Studying Scripture in small groups is not just Bible study—
not simply filling our brains with Bible trivia or proving and
protecting our pet doctrines. As followers of Jesus, we study
the Scriptures on Jesus' terms, not our own. This means that
we view and handle the Bible as God's Word just as Jesus did
(Matthew 4:4; 15:3-6). But our *reverence* for the Bible as God's

Word is only the beginning. As Jesus' followers, we must also *respond* to God's Word by living our lives on Jesus' terms.

Some of Jesus' religious contemporaries regarded the Scriptures as God's Word, and yet they rejected Jesus. To them Jesus said,

> You search the Scriptures because you think that in them you have eternal life; and it is they that bear witness about me, yet you refuse to come to me that you may have life. (John 5:39-40 ESV)

All our knowledge of the Scriptures is stagnant and lifeless without submission to Jesus in all areas of our lives. Our knowledge of God's Word is never meant to be a substitute for life-giving obedience to Jesus. Instead, the narratives, commandments and examples in God's Word give shape to our obedience to Jesus. As a follower of Jesus, Rebecca responded with greater faithfulness to Jesus when the Word was applied to an area of her life.

Like those we lead, small group leaders are called to prayerful, passionate, faithful submission to Jesus that is shaped by God's Word. Additionally, small group leaders have the joy, privilege and responsibility to usher those they lead into life-giving obedience to Jesus through the study and application of God's Word.

OPEN TO GOD'S FRESH WORD: INDUCTIVE BIBLE STUDY

Some students of Scripture walk around with *hoopty Bibles.* Hoopties are old, high-mileage cars. Their parts are held together by Crazy Glue, duct tape, cobbled parts from other hoopties and daily appeals to God. Hoopty Bibles are similar; they have so much highlighting that they look like they were stolen from the tester station at the Crayola factory. Scribbled notes, cracked spines and disintegrated covers point to habitual use. Hoopty Bible owners, like their hoopty car-owning counterparts, wear their Bibles like a badge of honor.

Whether or not students of Scripture scribble in their Bibles, most students of Scripture carry Hoopty Bibles around *in their heads*. Certain Bible passages call to our minds related sermons, teachings or personal studies. The ability to recall previous insights into certain Scripture passages is in fact a large part of how we internalize the Word of God. These insights serve as established, familiar paths that help us—and for centuries have helped other Christians—to find our way around in the Scriptures.

It takes time to locate these paths. Over time, though, we learn by these paths to quickly apply certain Scripture passages to our life situations. However, such familiarity can backfire on us, instilling within us a "been there, done that" attitude that closes our hearts off to fresh insights and applications that God desires to give us. Those of us who are newer to the practice of Scripture study may be less prone to this kind of familiarity, but all of us can be tempted to isolate certain passages from the texts in which they are situated. When we do so, we miss out on the full meaning of what the authors were communicating.

How do we walk down recognizable theological pathways in our heads *and* listen for fresh messages from the Spirit of God? Can we have our cake and eat it too? (Mmmmm . . . cake.) The short answer is, "Yes, we can!" We do this by studying the Scriptures *inductively.*[1]

---

[1]In preparing the Bible study material that follows, I benefited greatly from tools and concepts developed by Evan Keller, Bob Grahmann and Lindsay Olesberg. For more Bible study material go to <www.intervarsity.org/Biblestu/page/ Bible-studies-index>.

Inductive Bible study is designed to empower small groups and individuals to deeply and honestly examine what a biblical text is communicating on its own terms. We examine particular words, images and concepts in a given text to arrive at its central theme. This is different from deductive thinking. In a court case, the prosecution and the defense come with predetermined positions. They present and interpret evidence to suit those positions and to achieve a desired verdict. To *start with a conclusion* and to use the evidence to prove that conclusion is what is involved in deductive discovery.

A jury, however, attempts to objectively use all the evidence presented by the prosecution and the defense to arrive at a verdict. To *objectively gather, interpret and apply* all the evidence is what is involved in inductive discovery.

In a courtroom setting, the judge keeps the prosecution, the defense and the jury on task by pointing out

- what evidence *is* important to the case
- what evidence *is not* important to the case
- what courtroom procedures need to be followed
- how legal terminology ought to be understood

Small group leaders have something in common with judges: We remind group members to faithfully locate their interpretations of the passage in the biblical text. The secret to inductive Bible study lies in three letters: *OIA*. Three letters. Nice and painless. Piece of cake.

OIA

At the heart of inductive Bible study is *observation, interpretation* and *application.* The small group's initial exploration of a biblical passage is the *observation* mode; the jury is examining the evidence. The small groups' attempt to unravel the central truth of a biblical passage is the *interpretation* mode; here the jury interprets the evidence. During the *application* mode the jury's verdict is delivered; the small group grasps how to put into practice what they have gleaned from the passage. These different phases of study naturally build on each other: we can't interpret what the Scriptures mean until we look at what they say, and if we truly want to apply what we learn from them, then we have to correctly interpret what we find there.

OBSERVATION MODE

The observation mode helps us to fix our minds on a particular passage of Scripture. The observation mode helps those who are unfamiliar with the passage get acquainted with it. Meanwhile, for those who are familiar with the passage, the observation mode gets away from a "been there, done that" mentality. The legwork we do in the observation mode is called the *observation exercise*. Good observation exercises engage the imaginative and analytical parts of group members' minds. We lead creatively to connect group members with the people, places, images and situations in a biblical passage. It is through these connections that we begin our journey to the passage's core message.

Some observation exercises are better than others. Small group leaders must ask themselves, *Does this exercise drive us deeper into the biblical text?* They ought to evoke interest and focus, but if they don't cause us to engage the Scriptures, then we will miss out on the clues to the passage's meaning. Table 5.1 illustrates the difference between helpful and unhelpful observation exercises.

All kinds of observation exercises can be imaginative and creative. But only those exercises that help us to engage and

Table 5.1. Helpful and Unhelpful Observation Exercises in Three Biblical Passages

Passage	Genesis 2:4-25	Revelation 1	John 3:1-22
Helpful observation exercises • are rooted in Scripture • engage the creative/imaginative and analytical/logical parts of the mind • explore and analyze the Scriptures	Put yourself in the shoes of the man or the woman. What do you see, hear, taste and feel in the Garden of Eden? Make a list of the things that the humans are responsible for in the garden. Write a job description for employment in the Garden of Eden.	Concentrate on the scene in verses 9-20. If you were John, how might your recollection of Jesus in his earthly ministry be the same as/different from this vision of Jesus? Catalog the ways that the senses of sight, touch and sound are engaged in the passage. List the different images used to describe the church in the passage. What are some privileges and responsibilities associated with these images?	Explore the passage using some basic grammar tools like repetition of words, comparison/contrast (for example, "born of flesh" versus "born of Spirit") and cause/effect (for example, "He gave his one and only Son" [cause]; "so that everyone who believes in him will not perish" [effect]).
Unhelpful observation exercises • can be creative or thoughtful but don't motivate exploration of the passage • neglect the main point of a passage in favor of advancing an opinion	Imagine what it would be like to be naked in the Garden of Eden. How would this affect the way you did your work in the garden (especially with the animals)? If you were the man or the woman, what would it be like to hang out with God face to face? Discuss.	If Jesus appeared in this way to you, how would you react? Compare the suffering of missionary Jim Elliot with John's testimony of suffering for the gospel.	Think back to your own water baptism. If you could speak with Nicodemus, how would you persuade him to be water baptized in accordance with Jesus' command?

explore the passage are ultimately helpful. The simple observation exercise for John 3:1-22 in table 5.1 is not flashy, but exploring a passage grammatically does more to help us stick to the passage than speculation about water baptism. In fact, focusing on grammatical analysis of passages can be comfortable and constructive in the early stages of a small group. However, being that grammar analysis is logic-driven observation, you might want to work at more creative methods of observation so as to engage the imaginations of your group members.

THE INTERPRETATION MODE

Ideally, group members make fruitful observations of the passage and are ready to start drawing initial conclusions about the text's meaning. This brings us to interpretation mode. Members begin to advance points of view based on the things they encountered in the passage. Small group leaders can put forth questions that steer group members to a good interpretation. Good Bible study questions

- promote discussion, have multiple answers and are open-ended
- lead students of the Bible back into the text
- use language of the group and of the text
- vary in type and scope
- are creative and insightful, with answers that are not totally obvious
- are short and concise
- connect to and build on other questions

Bible study expert Bob Grahmann has identified four helpful types of questions for interpretation mode.

1. Questions that help the group to enter the scene.

2. Questions that highlight the tension or point of intrigue in a text.

3. Questions that connect our lives to the text.

4. Questions that link different portions of the discussion.

Table 5.2 illustrates the difference between helpful and unhelpful interpretation questions.

By the end of your time in the Scriptures, your group will have had a fruitful discussion that has gone in many different (and rewarding) directions. To bring all the pieces together, it is good to summarize what the group has discovered, to gather all the useful snippets of the discussion and fit them nicely into a big picture. Summaries can range from one sentence to a short paragraph. The passages in tables 5.1 and 5.2 might be summarized as follows:

- Genesis 2:4-24: God created humans for creative work, interdependent relationships and freedom through obedience to his commands.

- Revelation 1: In being called by God to be his priestly witnesses, Jesus' followers sometimes suffer at the hands of the world, but Jesus manifests his power among us.

- John 3:1-22: Our knowledge about Jesus, though accurate, is never a substitute for running toward his light to have more of us exposed and more of Jesus revealed.

Obviously, entering a passage, feeling the tension and understanding where the text intersects with everyday life requires diligent preparation and prayerful study on the part of the small group leader! While having several questions prepared is a good idea, plan to limit discussion to four interpre-

Table 5.2. Helpful and Unhelpful Interpretation Questions

Passage	Genesis 2:4-24	Revelation 1	John 3:1-22
Helpful interpretation questions • are rooted in the text • drive group members back into the text • don't have only one answer • vary in form from one another • link the text to everyday life	What does God's creation of the man tell us about the man's connection to God and the earth? In verses 16-17, what is the nature of the man's freedom? How does God-given freedom differ from how we conceive of freedom? What do God's motivations for creating the woman (v. 18) tell us about how God wants the man and the woman to relate to one another?	What light do John's circumstances (v. 9) shed on what it means to be blessed by God (v. 3) and priests for God (v. 6)? What does John's vision in verses 12-20 convey about Jesus? How does this picture of Jesus confirm/challenge how you experience him? Compare/contrast John's interaction with Jesus in verses 17-20 with that of "all the tribes of the earth" in verse 7. How does this inform the way we bear witness to Jesus in the nonbelieving world?	What does Nicodemus know about Jesus (v. 2)? For Jesus, why is Nicodemus' knowledge insufficient for seeing and entering the kingdom of God? In comparing himself with the snake that Moses lifted up (Numbers 21), what is Jesus saying about himself? What is the connection between believing in Jesus and loving the light?
Unhelpful interpretation questions • read into passages theological ideas that aren't there • invite speculation that doesn't originate in or lead back to the text • miss key points on the passage • don't foster discussion • ignore context	What do we learn about male headship in the family from this passage? (reads a particular theology into the passage) If the world was perfect, why would God need the man to care for the garden (vv. 5, 15)? (invites speculation that doesn't come from or lead back to Genesis 2)	Why do God's blessings always seem to come with suffering? (misses the point of Revelation 1 regarding blessing and suffering) How scary do you think it will be to face Jesus on the Day of Judgment if you are unsaved? (invites speculation that doesn't come from or lead back to Revelation 1)	What do you think the Pharisees told Nicodemus to ask Jesus? (invites speculation that doesn't come from or lead back to John 3) Snakes are usually bad in the Bible. Why do you think Jesus is comparing himself with one? (doesn't adequately explain the imagery; fails to deal with the context of Numbers 21)

tation questions. Doing so will ensure that the group dives deeply into the Word while honoring the time commitments of small group members.

Having been led by the Holy Spirit in observation, interpretation and summary, the small group's task is not yet complete. To accomplish the broader purposes of group Bible study, the group must determine what the passage is saying to individual members and the group as a whole.

THE APPLICATION MODE

"Blessed is the one who *reads the words* of this prophecy, and blessed are those who *hear it* and *take to heart what is written in it,* because the time is near" (Revelation 1:3, emphasis mine). Just as it did two thousand years ago, John's exhortation finds a home in gatherings where God's Word is read by God's people. In all three modes of inductive Bible study, we read and hear God's Word, but it is in the application mode that we concentrate on taking God's Word to heart through specific action.

In the application mode Jesus' role as the great and compassionate Judge of his people and the world is underscored. Throughout the Bible study he moves our hearts to respond to his Word and his presence with action. Without active, practical responses to Jesus, all of our Scripture study is meaningless, theological babble that has an appearance of godliness but denies its power (2 Timothy 3:5).

Our responses take many forms: We repent, we worship, we receive encouragement, we become reconciled to those we have wronged or who have wronged us, or we commit to action. No matter what the form, good response questions

- help us to respond to the main message of the passage

- are appropriate and rooted in God's will and character

- are concrete and personal

- can be accomplished with the empowerment of God and God's people

In other words, don't settle for vague applications like "Jesus is calling us to be nicer to other people." This may be true, but if by "other people" Jesus means my roommate, and if by "nicer" he means I need to ask for my roommate's forgiveness for something I did, then a better application would be "Jesus is calling me to ask for my roommate's forgiveness." Small group leaders must not be afraid to bring in applications that are specific to the group. If the group needs to be encouraged or if something already present in the life of the group is praiseworthy, then feel free to craft application questions that are in line with encouragement or praise. If the group needs to be admonished or challenged, then craft application questions that are in line with admonition or challenge.

Don't forget, however, that you are a member of the group; as a leader of the small group, you bear equal responsibility for its accomplishments *and* shortcomings! The Messiah has no use for small group leaders with messiah complexes. Even the prophets in the Old Testament identified with those to whom God had sent them. Also, remember to maintain an atmosphere of trust and openness in the group. You may have in mind particular applications for specific group members, but unless that application is praiseworthy or the member brings it up on their own in the group setting, such particular applications should be saved for a one-on-one conversation. There you can deal with a potentially difficult matter with the compassion and discretion to which we are called.

As with the interpretation questions, it's good to have several application questions ready and to choose one or two that fit with the discussion the group has had. Think through whether or not your group needs to process their responses or pray through them: some responses require that we simply agree with God and prayerfully do what he says, while others require that we seek out guidance and clarity from fellow Christians. You can have people respond individually, in pairs, or as a whole group. Table 5.3 illustrates some helpful and unhelpful application questions.

The rigorous application of God's Word to all areas of our lives is God's desired fulfillment of our faithful observation and interpretation of the Scriptures. In this way, the small group as "jury" submits itself to the wisdom and majesty of God our Father and Judge.

FEED YOURSELF FIRST:
PREP LIKE YOUR LIFE DEPENDS ON IT

Whether the event is a wedding reception or a Superbowl party or a catered fundraiser for Save the (insert your favorite cute, endangered animal here), everyone is afraid to be the first person to step up to the buffet line for food. You could be so hungry that you'd eat a porcupine and its momma, but you would still hide your grumbling stomach. Why? Because even when their stomachs are oinking, people don't want to look like pigs.

When preparing to lead an inductive Bible study, however, I exhort you in the name of Jesus: pig out. Feast on God's Word. Leaders of God's people are called by our Father to take God's Word to heart before bringing it to bear on the lives of those we lead. Like Ezekiel the prophet, who during a vision was called by God to eat God's words before speak-

Table 5.3. Helpful and Unhelpful Application Questions

Passage	Genesis 2:4-24	Revelation 1	John 3:1-22
Helpful applications • are concrete and specific • underscore the major point of the passage • invite group members to draw support from one another • reassure members of the empowerment of the Spirit of God • allow group members to share ideas with one another	Do you have any situations in which you're feeling particularly burdened or frustrated? How might someone help maximize your creativity and lighten your load?	In what ways do you need to experience the presence of Jesus to encourage you in evangelism? Are there things our small group can do to be of help in this area?	What are some regular disciplines that expose you to the light of Jesus? Which discipline do you find best opens you to Jesus' light?
Unhelpful applications • aren't concrete • have little to do with the main message of the passage • don't bridge the language of the text and the lives of group members	What are the qualities of a godly mate?	Have you experienced Jesus in the way that John did?	What has believing in Jesus been like for you lately?

ing them to Israel (Ezekiel 2:8—3:3), we are called to apply God's Word to ourselves before leading others in the observation, interpretation and application of biblical passages. By doing so we

- remain in loving submission to our Father and thereby avoid the pride of believing ourselves superior to those we lead

- gain firsthand knowledge of how God uses his Word to transform lives

- are prepared to offer our small group members not only our Bible study skills but also our biblically formed characters

Good small group leaders allow the Lord to work through his Word to heal, encourage, rebuke and challenge us. God holds his leaders to a strict standard (James 3:1; Hebrews 13:17), so affording him the opportunity to examine our hearts and to perform a work of grace in us prior to our service to others puts our leadership in perspective: We are first and foremost God's servants; serving others never trumps our service to him.

GOD'S FRUITFUL WORD AND THE ABUNDANT LIFE

My small group's study of Genesis 2 just kept bearing fruit. While Rebecca was wrestling with the implications of the text for her relationship with a non-Christian, a group member named Jacob told me that he would like to talk. Our one-on-one discussion a few days later was filled with stories of habitual sexual sin and a deep desire for lasting change. Jacob accepted that he would have to cut off sinful, destructive relationships, but he couldn't imagine how he would do so. Grounded in the Genesis 2 portrait of permanent, dignifying relationships, Jacob and I began to chart the new relational pathways our Father was carving out for him. As we talked, it became apparent that Jacob had never truly surrendered his life to Jesus. I led Jacob in a prayer in which he acknowledged Jesus' right to rule every aspect of his life.

One Bible study had produced an orchard's worth of fruit, and my mustard-seed faith (and my tactlessness) had received a workout. Studying Scripture in small groups is not about filling our brains with Bible trivia. Nor is it about proving and protecting our pet doctrines. It is about the kind of transformation that Jacob and Rebecca experienced when we observed, interpreted and applied Genesis 2 together. It's about allowing the Living God to bring his Word to bear on our lives so that we look more like Jesus.

Say it to yourself as many times as you need to, Mr. or Mrs. Small Group Leader:

It's not just a Bible study.

It's not *just* a Bible study.

It's *not* just a Bible study.

It's not just a *Bible* study.

It's not just a Bible *study.*

It's not just a Bible study.

Amen.

6

PRAYER AND WORSHIP
IN SMALL GROUPS

Úna Lucey-Lee

OUR LEADER SPREAD OUT a huge world map on the floor, pointed to a country and told the group that we were going to pray for Albania. I wondered if anyone else in the group had ever heard of Albania but thought it best not to do an impromptu survey in case I was the only one who had not. I was not quite ready to unveil my geographical ignorance to my new friends.

Albania. There it was on the map. Next to Greece.

I shifted my legs in their cross-legged position seeking the elusive comfortable spot on the floor. The leader told us that before 1944, Albania had been a predominantly Muslim country. After World War II the communist government set out to create the first atheistic country. No religious observance was allowed. Churches, mosques, monasteries and other religious institutions were closed, and foreign missionaries were expelled. Many Albanian clergy and religious citizens were imprisoned or put to death. Producing, distributing or possessing religious literature was a crime resulting in imprisonment. Albanians with Christian names were required to change them. Some ninety towns named after Greek Orthodox saints received different names.

After hearing this intense history, we were invited to pray. This was new to me—sitting around a world map with some people I barely knew and together asking God to bring freedom and life to a nation that was unknown to me. I had never asked God to get involved in a whole country, much less a country with such a concerted plan to keep God out. I remember thinking about prayer being both a duty and a privilege, and these thoughts led to questions, which quickly led to some silent misgivings about what we were doing.

We bowed our heads and started to pray. I listened to others and joined in thanking God for his love for all people. *Yes, that's true. God loves everyone in the world.* Others asked God to make an opening for the gospel in Albania and to sustain a remnant of his people. *Yes, it's true. The apostle Paul wrote about the gospel not being chained.* After about five minutes of fervent prayer, I assumed we were done and waited for the leader to say, "Amen." But much to my dismay, the prayer time continued for a while longer, as others in the group asked God for additional things or repeated what had already been said. A few times I had to open my eyes to stay alert; I stared at the map hoping to generate some original and inspired prayers of my own.

I would be lying if I said that I was eager and overflowing with faith during these prayer times. There was nothing particularly action-packed about what we were doing; we had a map, some information and a call to prayer. Fast-forward to December 1990 when the Albanian government's forty-year prohibition of religious observance was lifted. I was stunned. I was humbled. I was changed.

Somehow and in his way, God got involved and brought religious freedom to the people of Albania. You better believe that I attributed God's activity in part to that group of people asking him to get involved. I marveled at the idea that God listened to his people and took our requests seriously. Praising God for his work in Albania was a no-brainer.

Prayer and worship are connected. We collaborate with God and participate in his mission through a community appeal to him. During prayer, we worship by speaking about God's character. He is powerful, loving, generous, holy and just. When we witness God's transforming work in others in response to our prayers, it is natural to then give glory to God again. This further motivates us to persevere as a community in the work of prayer, where we seek God's deeper influence and glory in the world. The cycle from prayer to worship continues.

Unfortunately, this description of prayer and worship does not match many of the small groups of which I have been a part. Instead of planning for times of prayer and worship, many small groups limit prayer to the first few moments and the final two minutes of a meeting, before everyone rushes out the door to get home. More often than not, a group's worship together is limited by whether anyone can play a musical instrument, because many equate worship with singing. It is my hope that this chapter will show the integral role of a small group leader in making prayer and worship positive and transformative beyond a few moments and a couple of songs.

PRAYER

One of my favorite images about prayer comes from Hebrews 4. At the end of the chapter, the writer illustrates our privilege of approaching God's throne with the confidence that we will receive mercy and grace. I love the picture of coming to God with the expectation that he will distribute favor and kindness. We can confidently go to God and make requests of him because he is generous and hospitable. Jesus understands our unique human limitations and is full of resources to provide for our needs. It reminds me of borrowing an egg from my neighbor. I fully expect that if she has an egg, then she will give it to me—because I know her to be generous. The book of Hebrews uses language of royalty here, reminding me to revere the One of whom I make my requests and to remember that his rich supply of grace is inexhaustible. This invitation to approach God is extended to a group of people, and therefore it is the privilege of group leaders to guide their groups in coming near God in prayer and worship.

I believe God calls his people to pray and to give glory to him. Therefore we have a responsibility to do so. I point this out because in my sphere of ministry, I am not the go-to-gal for prayer and worship. My skills lie in other areas. But my stint praying for Albania taught me that God listens and responds to his people when they pray. I was changed by that experience. I think it is amazing that we can have a conversation with God where we both speak and we both listen. It is an honor and a responsibility to be included in God's transforming work in the world, and some of how that happens is through corporate prayer and worship.

Plainly put, prayer is communication between two parties: humans and God. It can be two-way communication between one person and God or a group of people conversing with God. Both parties are listening. Both parties are speaking. Prayer is *relational.*

We relate to God in prayer, and in group settings we relate

to one another. Sometimes we pray about concerns for individuals in the group or praise God for evidence of his presence in our life. In addition, we pray about needs of the larger community outside the small group, ranging from local to global needs, as well as give glory to God for the great things he has done. In the end, it is our pleasure to join with others in prayer and worship. Our experience of God's transforming work in concert with our prayers nurtures a small group's dependence on God and fuels community worship and desire for more partnership in prayer with God.

WORSHIP

Worship is associated with devotion. Like prayer, it involves communicating with God but it differs because of its focused recognition of God's superior character and work. Through worship we communicate to God our reverence, respect and love. Some worship features singing and other physical expressions to communicate this deference and respect to God. The task of a small group leader is to nurture devotion among those who attend and provide direction for acts of worship during the small group gathering.

Worship serves, additionally, to bring Christians into greater maturity of faith. I have experienced the touch of God while singing familiar worship songs. I have grown in my understanding of Jesus by singing hymns written in the nineteenth century. My ability to communicate gratitude to God has developed by being led to write and share a personal psalm in a group. My appreciation for God's work in the world has matured by learning praise songs in languages other than English. Moments spent focusing on one characteristic of God as described in a particular Bible passage have been powerful. A moment of silence within a group context has served to cement truth from God's word. The diversity of words, images, cadence, rhythm and style in these various experiences has expanded my view of God. My devotion to Jesus has been nurtured by these acts of worship and the leaders who guided me to them.

THE BIBLE ON PRAYER AND WORSHIP

I have long loved the name Cornelius because of its association to my paternal grandfather, an uncle, a few cousins and my eldest brother. As luck would have it, Cornelius made it into the Bible! In Acts 10 he is described as a devout man who feared God, gave money to the poor and prayed habitually. A military leader who operated with a chain of command, Cornelius understood God as a supreme leader who listens to the requests of his people. Through a series of parallel experiences involving prayer, angels and visions, God orchestrated a meeting between Cornelius and the apostle Peter, which was unexpected given the longstanding racial division between Jews and Gentiles. The result of this meeting was a major paradigm shift for Peter about the inclusion of the Gentiles among the people of God.

Normally I have focused on the divine brilliance in addressing racial prejudice and division and have missed a more subtle point in the narrative. Cornelius was praying at about three in the afternoon, a time of day which, as the writer of Acts earlier indicated, was designated for prayer (Acts 3:1). This suggests that prayer was a habit for Cornelius. During this regular time of prayer a messenger of God addressed Cornelius, assuring him that God had heard him. This got me wondering: how many times did Cornelius settle in to pray and get up to go back to work without any celestial visitation? How many weeks, months or years had he prayed at that hour? Did he ever get bored or lack verve? Did he ever wonder whether God heard him or not? I am inspired that behind the phenomenal juxtaposition of Cornelius and Peter's lives in the book of Acts is the backstory, that Cornelius's very ordinary habit of praying led to his being involved in a powerful work of God.

Testimonies of the integral practice of prayer and worship among the people of God go back as far as the Bible will take us. Some passages in the Bible state simply that a small group of people gathered and prayed. The book of Acts records communities praying together in times of trouble, at set hours for prayer, in commissioning others for ministry and when seeking direction for a decision. One of the first tasks of the early Christians was to select a leader to replace Judas. The community prayed for direction from God, whom they believed knew the hearts of all and was capable of revealing his preferences. As the early community grew to some five thousand people, they continued in their devotion to prayer and praising God together. Acts later describes individuals in the community who would go together to the temple for set times of prayer. The writer of Acts draws connections between a prayer meeting at Mary's house and Peter's miraculous release from jail via an angelic escort. One of my favorite events in the book of Acts is the birth of the Philippian church by the side of a river where people had gathered to pray. The clear testimony in Acts is that God's people participated together in prayer and worship.[1]

It is striking to me how many of the Bible's instructions and promises are addressed to the community of God but are typically read as applying only to me, myself and I. Perhaps I am not alone in this? Studying the Bible together can confront

---

[1] These various episodes of prayer appear in Acts 1:14, 24; 2:42, 47; 3:1; 12:1-17.

this misreading. We can turn our communal attention to God, seeking grace to live together according to the Scriptures and to express gratitude for his sustaining presence. Prayer and worship are ways to communicate to God about what the group is learning through Bible study.

Bible study, particularly when done in private, can sometimes be cerebral and analytical. Practicing group prayer and worship can address this imbalance with more intuitive and fluid rituals. These experiences that utilize different learning domains and create space for spiritual transformation to take place. Folks in your group who prefer a linear approach to life will grow by learning how to express themselves with more spontaneity. Those who might struggle with the learning styles most often associated with Bible study will feel free to communicate to God in prayer and worship without having to give a reason for everything they are saying.

PREPARING TO LEAD SMALL GROUP PRAYER AND WORSHIP

As I entered college, I was experiencing renewal in my life with God that was accompanied by a keen interest in the Bible. I eagerly signed up and anticipated the first meeting of a small group Bible study that met in my university residence hall. After the Bible study segment of the meeting was over, the leader instructed us to share prayer requests. I listened intently to everyone's concerns and was gearing up to pray. When it came time to pray, I told Jesus how great he was and asked him to get involved in every single, solitary request mentioned by my new friends. I kept praying for quite some time.

A few days after the study, the group leader chastised me for not praying in *the right way*. Evidently, I should not have prayed so long. I should not have prayed a monologue. I should have let other people pray for a few things. My prayers were tedious to the leader and, she inferred, to the rest of the group.

I was stunned. I was embarrassed. I sincerely did not know there was *a right way* to pray in groups. I am inclined to pay attention to directions, at least the first time I do anything, and I did not remember ever *hearing* of a right way. You can bet that I stayed within the leader's praying parameters from that point on. I was intent on learning to pray in groups.

While the practice of prayer and worship in a small group can be a flashpoint for differences in people's prior experiences, practices, values and opinions, it can also provide richness in experience and transformation for everyone. A good small group leader will prepare how to lead the group through this.

The temptation for the small group leader will be to downplay or ignore differences in people's perception due to the huge potential for chaos. On the other hand, you might be tempted to prescribe *the right way*. It will be vital to resist both temptations and instead navigate and guide the group in the midst of this diversity so that everyone can feel at home in the group even as each person is learning new things about prayer and worship.

In my case, our group was gathering for the first time and needed leadership throughout the meeting. My leader would have saved me from an embarrassing situation and directed the whole group in a positive prayer experience by communicating the prayer parameters *before* we started praying. But even a group that has gathered for a longer time will still look to the leader to provide some structure as the group welcomes new people and experiments with diverse methods and styles of prayer and worship. As long as your leadership is flexible, the group will experience safety and freedom in community prayer times.

One of the first steps in your preparation as a leader is increasing your knowledge and appreciation of different prayer and worship practices. This can be learned through talking with friends about their understanding of prayer and worship in small groups. You might also consider having a conversation in your small group where folks share about their experiences and beliefs about prayer. Often I will ask someone in the group to *lead* the group's prayer or worship. The only limits I place on this person are (1) the time allotted to each segment and (2) that a clear connection is made to the group's Bible study. This both gives a leadership opportunity to someone else in the group and grows the group's appreciation for various practices of prayer and worship.

You can also increase your exposure to different prayer and worship practices by participating in services or other ministry events with Christian communities that are unlike your own. Observe how prayer and worship is led in these settings, how the parameters are communicated, how the people are brought into the experience, and consider how elements of the practices you've observed might be transferred into your setting. Doing so has increased my own appreciation for the great diversity in how different communities respond to the call to prayer and worship.

Another tool at your disposal is time. Initiate conversations outside the group meeting to guide individuals in the group toward a satisfying prayer and worship experience for everyone. Even though the experience of my leader challenging my prayer monologue was not pleasant, her talking with me outside of the group time about group dynamics was helpful in reasserting the goal of approaching God in prayer and worship together as a group.

FOCUSING GROUP PRAYER AND WORSHIP

During an animated discussion with some colleagues about prayer on campus, we each shared our mental image of "quality prayer meetings." When we finally boiled down all the different ideas to the ingredients for a quality prayer meeting, the conclusion was that it had to not be boring or drag on too long. This, in a nutshell, reveals the tough thing about leading prayer. Sometimes it is ordinary and feels like anything except divine conversation with the almighty God. While you may not be able to guarantee that your small group prayer is never boring, however, with some preparation you can ensure that it is focused.

Prayer is relational. Daily newspapers or newsmagazines can inform group prayer by creating awareness of others and the need for God's transforming work. Many missionaries send out regular ministry reports replete with prayer requests. Churches often communicate needs of members to the congregation. Some small groups adopt a missionary and consistently provide financial and prayer support. In addition to these sources, there are the ever present needs of small group members and their loved ones.

Worship, by contrast, is vulnerable to too narrow a focus. Worship is not just singing; it includes any gesture toward God of honor or respect. The good news for people like me, who do not play an instrument or fancy the prospect of leading singing, is that there are many things a community can do to express honor and respect to God. You might lead the group in making collages that express praise for God's character. I have provided paper and pen for small group members to write a letter to God in which they can communicate devotion. Your group might make some type of memorial to God signifying important events in the life of your group. These are all creative ideas that a group can implement in lieu of music. However, if people in your small group play instruments, then utilize them as well. Delegating the worship leadership to group members from time to time could be a great growth opportunity for them. The practice of worship is one of devotion, of communicating blessing and reverence to God. This happens beautifully—but not exclusively—with the assistance of music and song.

"When you are done reading your Bible and getting ready to pray," my friend shared in a training exercise, "don't change subjects." Oftentimes we read God's Word and then ramble on in prayer about completely unrelated topics. This can happen in a group's worship as well. But if we believe God speaks through his Word, then God may have started a conversation in your small group during your time of Bible study. Your task as a leader is to usher in the rest of that conversation during prayer and worship. This is not to say that you should not pray about other things, but do pay attention to the connection between Bible study, prayer and worship.

THE END OF PRAYER AND WORSHIP

Everyone was itching to go when the leader informed our group that it was time to pray. We shared our personal items and needs of some other individuals outside our group. The leader set the parameters for our prayer time, adding "After an appropriate amount of awkward silence, I'll end our prayer time together." We all laughed, closed our eyes and bowed our heads. True to his word, once the silence approached uncomfortable, he said "Amen" and we were on our way.

This offhand comment typifies some attitudes and experiences of group prayer. While many know that they should pray, few seem to find it easy to navigate. It should come as no surprise, then, that in the Bible, prayer is often associated with perseverance. My experience has taught me that with good leadership, small group prayer and worship can become a vital part of our time together and not the obligatory book-ends to a Bible study.

One of my favorite prayers in the Psalms is the request that God incline his ear to his people. It is a request for God to listen and pay attention. The beauty of my experience praying for Albania is that I experienced God paying attention and then getting involved in the world to bring freedom and trans-formation to others. I was led to this experience by someone with a map, some information and a call to prayer. His call to prayer became mine, and I now pass it on to you.

7

SHEPHERDING THE FLOCK

CARING FOR EACH SHEEP

Tina Teng

UNDERLYING THE MECHANICS of the "task" of small group leadership is the reality that you're leading people. What do you do when members give voice to pain and struggle? When someone in your small group is in real crisis? How do you care for each member individually and challenge them to grow—especially when they're each at different places spiritually? How do you go from running a meeting to leading a community of friends?

Small group leadership requires sensitivity, wisdom and God's help! The biblical metaphor of shepherding people as one shepherds a flock comes to mind: tending to the needs of individuals and the whole group, providing provision, protection and guidance to good pasture, and more—each in turn, and all at the appropriate time.

Much of what I know today about the internal work of shepherding a small group, I learned from one of four events in my life. Some lessons came during actual meetings, but frequently they came outside of the formal group time. As you read my story and the Bible passages that shaped each of these moments, it is my hope that God will shepherd *you*, and that as you live out these lessons, each one under your care will flourish.

WHEN PEOPLE GIVE VOICE TO PAIN AND STRUGGLE

Looking back, I don't know how I even knew where she lived. Or that it'd be good to talk to her. But there I found myself on the way home from church one chilly Sunday afternoon, not even halfway through my first semester at Harvard, ringing her doorbell. God guided me to her door for far greater purposes than I ever would have guessed.

My small group leader's roommates ducked out of the living room as I sat cross-legged in front of her, trying to give words to how disoriented I felt. Becoming just another drop in the ocean that is Harvard College was humbling and even at times humiliating, having been the big fish in the small pond I hailed from. Whether it had ever been true before, it was now painfully clear to me that I wasn't the smartest, hardest-working, nicest, prettiest or even "most Christian" person around. Stripped of all these labels I wore around in my head by a place I'd have to eventually call home, I didn't know who I was anymore.

She listened with full attention and asked gentle questions to better understand what I was thinking. She spoke words that reassured me that I wasn't a freak or a failure or at fault for feeling the way I did. She wasn't bothered by the tissues soggy with shame. My eyes closed, I listened closely to her as she read a passage of Scripture—Isaiah 40—that I'd never heard before, that spoke exactly to my situation.

Comfort, comfort my people, says your God.

Speak tenderly to Jerusalem, and proclaim to her that her hard service has been completed, that her sin has been paid for, that she has received from the Lord's hand double for all her sins. . . .

A voice says, "Cry out." And I said, "What shall I cry?"

"All men are like grass, and all their glory is like the flowers of the field. The grass withers and the flowers fall, because the breath of the Lord blows on them.

Surely the people are grass. The grass withers and the flowers fall, but the word of our God stands forever." . . . Do you not know? Have you not heard? The LORD is the everlasting God, the Creator of the ends of the earth. He will not grow tired or weary. . . .

Even youths grow tired and weary, and young men stumble and fall; but those who hope in the Lord will renew their strength. They will soar on wings like eagles; they will run and not grow weary, they will walk and not be faint.

After she finished reading that passage over me, she gave me an anchor, a word that wasn't comparative, merit-based or going to change in the next stage of life: beloved. God's beloved.

One of the easiest and most common things to do when people are sharing vulnerably about a difficult situation or a real hardship is to jump in and do a combination of problem-solving, judging or preaching. I've found this impulse in me whether I'm a small group leader or friend because I so much want to "fix" people's pain. But even though this reaction might genuinely emerge out of a desire to show love, it rarely demonstrates the sensitivity and empathy that a hurting person needs.

In listening to me, sharing that passage and that word with me and then praying with me, my small group leader modeled for me a very different response. I heard words of comfort and healing, and then she blessed me and I was sent forth. In the same way, Jesus cared for people in pain. He demonstrated as much in a dramatic encounter in Mark 5 with a hemorrhaging woman:

> A large crowd followed him and pressed in on him. Now there was a woman who had been suffering from hemorrhages for twelve years. She had endured much under many physicians, and had spent all that she had; and she was no better, but rather grew worse. She had heard about Jesus, and came up behind him in the crowd and touched his cloak, for she said, "If I but touch his clothes, I will be made well." Immediately her hemorrhage stopped; and she felt in her body that she was healed of her disease. Immediately aware that power had gone forth from him, Jesus turned about in the crowd and said, "Who touched my clothes?" And his disciples said to him, "You see the crowd pressing in on you; how can you say, 'Who touched me?'" He looked all around to see who had done it. But the woman, knowing what had happened to her, came in fear and trembling, fell down before him, and told him the whole truth. He said to her, "Daughter, your faith has made you well; go in peace, and be healed of your disease."

Although he's at the center of a crowd of people and on his way to save a dying little girl, Jesus notices an anonymous touch to his cloak and cares to figure out who touched him. Because of her physical condition, this woman would have been considered "unclean" and a social outcast—the kind of woman you ignore. But Jesus allows his path to be diverted and gives her his full attention. The whole story tumbles from her lips, and given that she's dealt with this for twelve years, it is not a short story. But Jesus listens. She, too, is beloved. And when he opens his mouth, he speaks words that commend her for her faith and confirm her healing. He blesses her and sends her to go in wholeness and freedom from her suffering.

HEAL, BLESS, SEND

Sitting in front of my small group leader that day, and reading this account of how Jesus interacted with the woman, I learned what to do when I'm with someone in pain. First, and most importantly, listen to the person, giving them your full attention. This begins the process of healing. Almost always, the main desire of the person sharing is your empathetic listening ear. You probably already know this to be true from your own experiences; when hurting, you just want to be understood and to have others sit quietly with you.

If it seems like the person is ready to hear your thoughts and invites your counsel, then *acknowledge* the difficulty of their situation—giving it its due weight and legitimacy. If you have a personal experience of how God ministered to you in a similar situation, share that story. If there's a passage of Scripture attached to that memory for you, share that passage to encourage them and cast a different light on their situation. Don't feel the need to produce something personal to share, however. Sometimes we can't easily identify with a person giving voice to pain, and there isn't a verse that immediately comes to mind. In those cases, it's appropriate to honestly recognize that—and that in itself can be a blessing.

After sharing encouragement and discussing everything pretty thoroughly, or after simply listening if you didn't have anything else to offer, ask if they'd like to pray together or receive prayer. Praying right then and there for the person in pain completes the work of blessing and starts the work of sending. As you pray, name the suffering and confusion for what it is. But also give voice to the deep hope that you have for their situation because of Jesus' power. Claim the sure promises of Scripture on behalf of the person.

"Heal, bless and send" is a short three-word reminder of what to do when offering prayer ministry to someone, but it isn't so much the magic formula to care for someone who's hurting as it is a reminder that Jesus *can* heal us, that *he* has a word or even many words of blessing for us, and that he *sends us forth* to live in freedom. As you care for those who speak to you of pain and struggle, don't stop after healing and blessing. Finish the work and send them forth to go and do the same.

I didn't follow in the footsteps of my small group leader and start leading small groups for quite some time. But the way God used her in my life did a whole lot in the meantime. That anchor she gave me changed the way I saw myself. That truth shaped the way I led worship for my college fellowship, that reality made me a better friend. This reminder of who I was helped me withstand far more difficult crises that arose afterward—and taught me what was at the core of the gospel for my non-Christian friends. In good time I became a small group leader. Knowing I was beloved by God—knowing that he could heal me, bless me and send me forth to be used by him—helped me love and care for each precious one in my small group in the same way.

FOLLOW UP ONE-ON-ONE

Javier had been recommended to take over co-leading one of the men's small groups at our church in the new year. I had heard that he was one of the most committed members of the group, and the current co-leaders thought highly of him. I was only somewhat acquainted with him though, so as the church's small group coordinator I wanted to get to know him better before an official transition process began.

As I sat across from Javier at dinner before I was to visit their small group, I found things to be slightly less straightforward than I had anticipated. I was impressed with the way he spoke of wanting to grow spiritually; with quiet sincerity he told me just how much he valued his relationship with God. As the conversation eventually moved along to local public service opportunities, I listed for him some of the most valuable ministries and nonprofit organizations I knew of in the area. His response surprised me.

"I want to learn how to fly-fish though. I haven't heard of any community volunteer programs that do that with kids. Maybe I should just start my own."

Fly-fishing? The urban youth in Boston would have zero interest in fly-fishing, and he'd be hard-pressed to find a place close by where he could do that.

We moved on to talking about church. Unexpectedly, he announced his plans to switch churches the following year. I asked why, and he nonchalantly declared, "It's just not cool enough. I'm looking for something more." I was a bit stumped as to what to say. I knew him well enough to have invited him to hang out over dinner and to have that invitation enthusiastically accepted. I knew he was committed enough to the church to be planning on finishing out the year with his small group. However, I wasn't sure that our relationship was strong enough for me to be pretty direct with him. I thought he needed someone to challenge his self-oriented, consumerist mentality when it came to church and ministry, but that didn't mean I wanted to be the one to do it!

As I listened to Javier talk, more than anything I wondered what the trajectory of his life would be should no one ever confront him on his selfishness. I looked at my watch and knew that no matter which direction I tacked in conversation, we'd be late for the small group meeting. As I did my best to think on my feet, I also prayed, *God, you know that it's not about whether he stays in our church or not—or whether he agrees to co-lead the small group next year. Help me speak to the heart of the matter—and help this go well!*

"Javier, I totally hear you on these things—I think it's great you want to do more community service! It sounds like you haven't perfectly meshed with everyone at church, and that's been somewhat disappointing. But I just have to say that what I'm hearing from you has a whole lot more to do with *you*—and what you want—than about the people you'd like to serve or the people God puts you in relationship with, for your growth and for theirs. I know the other churches you're considering, and we're actually pretty similar in feel, though you should check them out for yourself no matter what. But the grass is *always* greener—whether it's your church now or your job situation later or whether even your friends are good enough for you. Whatever you decide is entirely up to you, but you just need to know that in life, it's actually *not about you*."

I took a deep breath and reached for my glass of water. I definitely hadn't invited Javier to dinner expecting this sort of conversation. My general impression had been that he was a humble, articulate and generally interesting guy. I had been glad for an opportunity to get to know him better. But as I sat waiting for him to respond, silently praying for God to work in his heart, I could see that he had taken what I said seriously. And I was grateful for having been given the opportunity to offer a different perspective and speak a word of challenge into his life.

He didn't end up saying much in response, and we closed out dinner aware that we'd had a real conversation and a pretty intense one at that. We rolled in a bit late to small group, and since he left halfway through, we didn't talk more after that. We were no longer attending the same service at church and so only saw each other in passing; our conversations were brief but cordial.

Three months later, he messaged me on Facebook, a short but meaningful set of sentences:

(no subject)
hey tina,
in retrospect, the conversation we had this year is the most important that i can remember.
this is a long time in coming, and i still don't really have things figured out, and i'm still pretty much a fringe individual by my own choosing. but even though i haven't come to any conclusions, i'm glad you were able to show me some tough love.
thinking of you,
javier

Reading his message, I felt gratefulness again for how God answers prayer, grateful for how God led me to speak honestly to Javier and for how God gave him a heart that was open to listening and changing. I had prayerfully taken a risk in confronting Javier and had chosen to trust God for the outcome. And I saw how God used a heart willing to partner with him to shepherd his people.

Most things never get fully addressed during a small group meeting. Small groups can be rather large, meeting times rather short, and some small group cultures are not the most conducive to going deep. It's critical then to have the time and availability in your schedule to make space for individual meetings where more personal growth and development can occur. In Javier's case, regular attendance didn't guarantee that his small group leaders really knew him and the ways God wanted to shape his character. They knew some of what was true for him but not so much about his deeper issues. My making the effort to get to know him outside of our normal context opened the door for greater transformation.

During early stages in the life of a small group, it's generally helpful to make broad efforts to draw people out since you're all just getting to know each other. But as time progresses and you begin to be more familiar with one another, observe how people engage one another. If the most talkative member of your group one day walks in sullen and withdrawn and leaves without making a contribution, check in to hear what is going on. Someone might casually mention a serious prayer request during sharing time and make light of it—or they might intentionally drop a bombshell that screams for some support. Either way, follow up! If appropriate, ask them directly if they could use some support and what would be helpful. If not, pull them discreetly to the side before they walk out the door at the end of the meeting. If they dash out before you can reach them, call or e-mail later on to get more of the back story and ask some clarifying questions. Set up coffee for the next day or plan to drop by their place. For some who are truly reticent and never seem to stray from their usual expression and demeanor, simply asking how they are doing every once in a while will express appropriate care and interest in their lives.

People can feel lost in the shuffle even in a small group context. Individuals in your small group flourish with attention and care. They need a shepherd who can leave the ninety-nine to seek them out. That would be you: meeting with people on a regular basis one-on-one or in small clusters strengthens relationships within the group and builds trust.

As a shepherd to your little flock, you're aiming for more than just camaraderie and friendship. You want to take your flock to good pasture so each grows healthy and strong, maturing and developing steadily. When you see dangerous predators out to eat your sheep, you leap to their defense. When there's a sprained ankle or a broken limb, you're one of the first responders—sometimes you have to set the bone! Meeting one-on-one offers you plenty of room (with plenty of reason) to take it beyond coffee and just getting to know you.

DISCERNING WHETHER CHALLENGE OR ENCOURAGEMENT IS NEEDED

Earlier on in my leadership of small groups, I was all about gentle encouragement. Some of that emerged out of my background as a Chinese-American woman who preferred indirect communication around sensitive topics and who took challenge and criticism better when it was preceded by affirmation. But I soon learned that while some people need gentle encouragement, others needed to hear critique and challenge straight, loud and clear. Javier really wouldn't have heard me if I had indirectly suggested that I thought he might be just a tad self-oriented in his motivations. But he certainly heard me when I was willing to look him in the eye and tell him that he needed to change.

If you don't *challenge* people to grow in their love for God, his purposes, his people and his Word, you lose out on helping people discover all that God has in store for them. If you don't also *encourage* people towards these things, you run the risk of them pursuing God out of a driven sense of inadequacy and a need to prove themselves—and losing out on the joy of relationship with a gracious Lord. Encouragement isn't necessarily gentle and soft and indirect; it can be given with great forcefulness. And challenge isn't necessarily harsh or difficult to hear; a challenging word can actually be quite kind and simple.

Jesus had that ability to shepherd individuals with insight into what each one needed to hear and how they would best receive it. Understanding the parable of the prodigal son in Luke 15 hinges on our ability to see that Jesus is speaking to two different audiences simultaneously and has tailored his message to each one. For the tax collectors and sinners who had gathered around to hear him, Jesus' portrayal of the younger son is an encouragement: a gracious Father will respond with a kiss and a forgiving embrace to any wayward "younger sons" who return home. For the Pharisees and the teachers of the law, Jesus' portrayal of the older brother is a message of challenge to these "older brothers" who have bitterly obeyed their father. They have never tasted the sweetness of being with God and resent the reunion of prodigals with their Father.

Ministering confidently to individuals in your small group one-on-one takes time and a lot of asking God for wisdom. You might wonder how and when to give what amount of challenge and encouragement. But don't get too hung up figuring that out. Learn about God's heart and the things he truly cares about—and trust him to convey through you the message he has for each one you speak with.

WHEN PEOPLE ARE IN CRISIS

Dolores was precious to me, but most of the time I had no clue how to be her small group leader. It seemed like she was constantly beleaguered by tremendously hard times, one following right after the other. First it was depression brought on by missing home terribly. She went home and gained a lot of weight. An eating disorder followed, accompanied by suicidal thoughts. This made it incredibly hard to focus on her academics, so Dolores was put on academic probation and took some time off of school. Being home was good at first, then became more difficult. Now, back at school, it seemed like things were finally looking up. She was steadily making friends and feeling a lot better about everything: her body image, academics, relationships and faith.

I was so proud of her returning to school and starting over, but when she told me about her plan to get silicone breast implants, I was against the idea for a number of reasons. So it was hard to figure out how to respond later on, when the deed was done and she was so obviously happy about it.

"You wanna see 'em?" Dolores stood in the hallway to my living room about to lift up her shirt.

I wasn't sure whether I wanted to see them. "Umm . . . I guess so!" I managed to muster up without too much of an awkward pause. The first thing I noticed was the scar tissue; it looked angry and red beneath her outstretched arms. She had stopped me from giving her a hug when I answered the door because of the pain and sensitivity. That reminded me of just how much Dolores had been through in the short three years I had known her.

I don't know what I first said in response. I think I was still in shock. But before she had arrived, I had asked God to show

me how to demonstrate the love he had for her without con-
doning what she had done.

Often when I thought about how to shepherd Dolores, John
10 came to mind. There Jesus calls himself the good shepherd who defends his flock from wolves, thieves and robbers
who come to attack and prey upon the sheep. "The thief
comes only to steal and kill and destroy," he said; "I have
come that they may have life, and have it to the full."

Once I saw her scars, I knew what to do. "Wait, just one
second," I told her, and I dashed to my bedroom and grabbed
two little jars sitting on my dresser before running back. "Scar
gel and cocoa butter. It'll help your scars heal faster and leave
less of a mark!" She smiled her thanks. This was a great way
to show that I cared about her and wasn't going to judge her
or stir up unnecessary anxiety about what was now done. The
scar gel and cocoa butter became a tangible expression of the
fact that God and I were about her healing and restoration.

Although I was on my own in that moment to figure out how
to love Dolores as I knew Jesus loved her, I had learned how
to do that over three years with her in a small group. The
women in that group had been committed to Dolores in all of
her ups and downs. The three of them rallied around Dolores
when she first shared about her inability to focus on her
schoolwork or even get out of bed in the morning. They scheduled themselves into her life—Charlotte would have breakfast
with her, Grace would go work out at the gym with her in the
afternoon, and Sheba helped her find a low-key part-time job
that involved cooking and hospitality, two activities she enjoyed that gave her life.

As the small group leader, I felt joy and great gladness that
I wasn't the only one at the center of her support network. Our
group had developed real love and concern for each other

and was a genuinely tight-knit community of friends. But the foundation for all of that was undeniably Christ. Over the past semester and a half, we had become a community that trusted each other. All five of us met regularly each week. When we looked at Scripture, we came with an eagerness to learn and grow. When we shared and prayed, we came with vulnerability and honesty. Over and above all, through the weeks of hanging out, talking about all aspects of life and our Christian faith and laughing over good snacks, we had tasted a bit of the "life to the full" Jesus offered in John 10. And we wanted more of that for each other. Without such a solid foundation in Christian community as a small group, none of our care for Dolores would have been possible.

KNOW YOUR LIMITS

Dolores had a great peer support network in our small group, and if she hadn't trusted us with the truth of what she was dealing with, I don't know where she'd be today. Some people's family backgrounds or church cultures stigmatize certain issues, leaving people unwilling or even afraid to admit they don't have it all together or need help. Some people will have tried to share their need with people who didn't know how to respond helpfully. An unhelpful past experience can make it harder to trust people with personal pain in the future. If your small group has established a high level of trust with each other, it may be the first and perhaps only place where someone feels truly safe to share what's going on.

But one of the most critical turning points in Dolores's path toward general well being was when we realized the limits of what we could do for her. We wanted to suggest getting professional care and mental health services to fully address the complex issues she was facing, but we didn't know how she would receive that suggestion. We prayed together about it before one of us, Sheba, brought it up with her. Sheba had struggled herself with depression in the past and could vouch for the effectiveness of the medications she took, and Charlotte, Grace and I had all had close friends or family members with mental health issues. Our own past experiences dealing with mental health treatment and care helped Dolores understand where we were coming from, but it was our demonstrated love and acceptance of her that caused her to listen to us.

As a small group leader, whatever your life stage, you will be faced with issues beyond your own wisdom and experience. It could be a member who has been assaulted or raped, someone with a substance abuse problem, a couple discussing divorce. These major life issues are beyond what you or your small group can and should take on.

With God's help, we can trust Christian community with our brokenness and desperate need for Jesus, and "confess [our] sins to each other and pray for each other . . . that [we] may be healed" (James 5:16). A need for healing may not always involve a sin to confess, but when complex areas of brokenness are brought to the Lord in the context of the group, and we begin to feel as though we're in over our heads, it's appropriate to rely on the strengths and resources of others. Local churches sometimes provide lists of Christian counselors, psychologists and social workers that you could refer your small group member to. Community health centers, university health services and corporate human resources departments could also be of help.

Sometimes group members don't need professional care but rather the wisdom of someone at a life stage ahead of you. One of my former small group members got married straight out of college but stayed in the area for graduate school. Fortunately for me, she joined my local church and we got to stay in touch and see each other every weekend. But her questions and struggles shifted to how to relate to her in-laws, how to buy a condo or how to manage a graduate school workload. I didn't have much to offer her as a single, rent-paying, nongrad-student friend!

Just as in Dolores' situation, I wasn't the only person she was looking to for support. There were other members in our small group community who were a step ahead of both of us and could speak into her life. And there was a church community around our small group that included older married folks with children and aging parents who could speak to the life-stages that were ahead of all of us. And in this intergenerational community of grandparents and toddlers, parents and teenagers—there was much wisdom to be shared as Jesus blessed us with "life to the full."

WHEN PEOPLE ARE AT DIFFERENT PLACES SPIRITUALLY

You'd think that opening your small group to a non-Christian would be a no-brainer, right? But no. Members of the small group Josh and I were co-leading had their concerns about including Tien.

"Jesus said go and make *disciples,* not converts. If we let non-Christians into our small groups, where will the 'safe spaces' be for Christians to talk about their problems and pray for their non-Christian friends?" This was from Raquel, our resident "theologian-in training." "That'll just be awkward," said Oscar, our talkative rambler who made most meetings somewhat uncomfortable himself. Monica smiled prettily and chirped, "Whatever you guys decide is fine with me, because I've got to go in five minutes anyhow!" as she adjusted her hair for the fourth time that hour.

"Imagine what it could be like," I responded, "if *all* our small groups were willing to include non-Christians. Evangelism and discipleship would happen side-by-side—and we'd stop seeing these things as mutually exclusive polar opposites."

"We *say* we're about 'bringing the whole gospel to the whole campus to transform the whole world,'" Josh jumped in to add, "but if we aren't even open to the five of us figuring out how to make space for Tien to join our small group, how are we supposed to live out our mission statement?"

"What *couldn't* we discuss openly if Tien were here, Raquel?" I jumped back in. "What topics would be off-limits or taboo? How else do we share life together if not by talking about everything openly? And c'mon, how cool would it be if Tien actually *became* a Christian?! That'd be great!!"

As it turned out, Tien didn't become a Christian that year. But the group did decide to include her, and we had a phenomenal year together. Tien's shy, quiet demeanor affected Oscar, and Oscar asked us how he could curb his cutting tones. His prayer request one day was for God to help him stop making rude remarks that hurt his sister and friends. Raquel's deep angst about complex matters of faith was reined in as she sought to explain the basics of the Christian faith to her new friend Tien. In doing so, she discovered what was at the core of the gospel and what wasn't. Monica was pressed to ask how deep her commitment to her spiritual growth was when Tien showed up more consistently and faithfully than she did.

Tien came close to conversion, committing herself to Jesus at our college fellowship's retreat midway through the year, but her parents objected and she backed off. Though we still pray for her to choose Jesus' approval over her parents' approval, we also thank God for how he used her so unexpectedly to help us all grow.

In the same passage where Jesus calls himself the good shepherd, he explains who he sees as his flock: "I have other sheep that are not of this sheep pen. I must bring them also. They too will listen to my voice, and there shall be one flock and one shepherd" (John 10:16). Jesus is not just about gathering up Christians; Jesus actively shepherds non-Christians and calls us to do the same by actively welcoming them into our small groups.

We can understand and accept this. What is sometimes difficult for us to believe is that Jesus might have something for *us* to gain in the process.

In his goodness, Jesus used our small group to continue drawing Tien to himself. But he also used Tien to challenge and refine the rest of us—no matter where we were in our spiritual walk. Jesus is always setting us up for incredible growth via unexpected means, obstacles and difficult conversations while still accomplishing his purpose in drawing those who don't know him to himself.

To welcome each person into your group means to make space for all of their different personalities, temperaments and levels of spiritual maturity. To do this in entirely Christian groups can be frustrating and difficult at times. Ironically, even though the idea of including non-Christians *feels* like that would be even more challenging, you might be surprised by how their presence actually puts everything in perspective. That's right, you might start to think, *this* is what God's kingdom work is actually all about—bringing other sheep into the sheep pen.

EVERY SHEPHERD IS A SHEEP

As you try to shepherd your little flock and face wolves, thieves and robbers of all kinds, you may doubt your shepherding abilities and wonder why you signed up for this responsibility. Sometimes in a conflict you'll have a hard time determining what the problem is all about. What was the presenting issue? What might be underlying that? Which should you deal with first? Or are you just imagining something's wrong when everything's okay? These are tough questions!

You are called shepherds and charged to be shepherds just like Jesus: overseers, servants, examples. God calls you to serve in that role with the right motivations, and this charge also comes with a promise:

> Be shepherds of God's flock that is under your care, serving as overseers—not because you must, but because you are willing, as God wants you to be; not greedy for money, but eager to serve; not lording it over those entrusted to you, but being examples to the flock. And when the Chief Shepherd appears, you will receive the crown of glory that will never fade away. (1 Peter 5:2-4)

There's a good reward in store for shepherds who oversee, serve and live as an example for their flock. This work you're doing has consequences well beyond the group's life—in your life and in theirs! You get a crown of glory, bestowed on you by the Chief Shepherd, who is the good shepherd. You are an under-shepherd, which means that each little one under your care never stops being under his ultimate care. Therefore, whenever you get concerned about anyone in your flock, you can just bring that person to him.

What's clear, though, is that this is not a job you can hold at a distance and run from when the going gets tough. Jesus addresses the bad under-shepherd in John 10 as well, from verses 11-13:

I am the good shepherd. The good shepherd lays down his life for the sheep. The hired hand is not the shepherd who owns the sheep. So when he sees the wolf coming, he abandons the sheep and runs away. Then the wolf attacks the flock and scatters it. The man runs away because he is a hired hand and cares nothing for the sheep.

Don't be a hired hand in your heart when you take on the role of being a small group leader or become one when challenges arise. But if you find that happening, take encouragement from another observation by Peter:

For you were like sheep going astray, but now you have returned to the Shepherd and Overseer of your souls. (1 Peter 2:25)

At the core, you're just a sheep yourself. The Shepherd took care of you well before you became a small group leader. And he continues to do so. Let that remind you that no matter how small, large, strong or strange your flock is, no matter how ill-equipped or capable you are or feel, above all, you are one of God's sheep—he is *your* shepherd. As you first allow him to tend to you, he can and will use you. You may make mistakes and fail, but you'll discover that even those things he can turn around and use for his own glory! This is the shepherd you have—powerful, perfect, strong and wise. Relax and trust his ultimate leadership.

8

SMALL GROUP EVANGELISM

Myron Crockett

NOTHING HAPPENED.

Having just prayed and read through Galatians 3:26—4:19, I was waiting for a bomb to go off in Julio's dorm room.

But nothing happened.

Hours earlier, while I had been putting the finishing touches on the study, a single thought knocked persistently on my brain: *You won't get through this Bible study tonight.*

Thinking this to be a demonic attempt to upset me, I prayed and mumbled something equivalent to "Knock it off, punked-out angelic wanna-be!"

In fact, a woman is going to have a problem with the phrase "sons of God" in Galatians 3:26.

When the thought got so specific as to pinpoint the exact verse someone would object to, I started to think that Jesus was speaking. After all, demons aren't known for warning us about upcoming complications in Bible study. But now we were about to start our journey into the text, and nothing had happened. Business as usual.

Until the knock on the door.

Julio opened the door. "Everyone, this is my friend Anezka." We would find out hours later that earlier that week Julio had invited Anezka, a Czech exchange student, to our small group.

For Anezka's benefit, we reread the passage. As I was leading the group into the study, Anezka interrupted. "Why does it say 'sons of God'? Why not 'daughters of God' or 'sons and daughters of God'?"

And that was the end of our Bible study for that night, just as the Spirit had predicted. But it was the beginning of evangelism.

To be honest, Anezka had a point. Galatians 3:26, 4:5, 4:6 and 4:7—"sons of God" was popping out from the first century and making us decidedly uncomfortable in the twenty-first. "It's just an example of the male oppression that is in Christianity. God is called 'Father.' Eve is blamed for eating the apple. No women writers in the Bible. Christianity oppresses women." Anezka quickly moved from opinionated to angry.

I was angry too. At Anezka. At Julio for inviting her. At Jesus. You don't prayerfully prep a Bible study just to get caught with your pants down. But I knew that if Jesus had anything to do with derailing the study, then he was also laying new railroad tracks.

For the next hour we talked (and argued) about women in the Bible: How Eve *and* Adam are implicated in Genesis 3; how the women among God's people (in the Old *and* New Testaments) fared far better than women in other cultures and religions; how female prophetesses spoke authoritatively in the Bible; how women were the economic backbone of Jesus' ministry—the first to bear witness to and testify about Jesus' resurrection, and leaders in the New Testament apostolic network.

But more significant than all this was the testimony of the female small group members. All of the women in the group piped up about their good, bad and ugly experiences in the church. For the first time that night, Anezka's hard shell showed some cracks.

"Why won't he talk to me? I ask him to show himself to me, and he won't talk to me." Tears came. For the next ninety minutes we told Anezka of how God had met us in very real, supernatural ways and how God loved her and wanted to have fellowship with her. By the time midnight rolled around, Anezka allowed us to pray for her. More tears and visible joy followed.

Anezka did not become a Christian that night, but many small group members would see her on campus, and they followed up with her. Eventually, small group members invited Anezka to a gospel concert at a local church. Amazingly, Anezka not only showed up but brought two of her fellow exchange students. Toward the end of the night, the church issued an invitation for non-Christians to place their trust in Jesus. One of Anezka's friends went up to talk to someone about following Jesus; apparently the person she spoke with gave her a prophetic word that was so undeniably specific to her life that she gave her life to Jesus that night.

If you're saying to yourself, *That kind of thing would never work with my group,* relax. If blind replication is what I was after here, then I would have to supply you with an angry but open Czech student, a dude named Julio and an eleven-person small group studying Galatians at the University of New Orleans in 2001. Just focus on how our small group took Anezka seriously and shared the good news of Jesus with her. Focus on how the collective witness of a network of Christians resulted in the salvation of one of Anezka's friends. Focus on how God worked supernaturally on Anezka's behalf through a mere invitation to a small group meeting. This kind of evangelistic potential rests within your own small group.

The secret to small group evangelism is God's work in and among Christian communities to carry the gospel to the unbelieving world.

THE *BIG* SECRET OF SMALL GROUP EVANGELISM

Evangelism is the *process* and the *event* of communicating the good news of Jesus Christ with people who do not yet follow Jesus. The goal of evangelism is for unbelievers to place their faith in Jesus and thereby be liberated from the sinful pattern of the world. Through faith in Jesus, we are reconciled to God our Father and empowered to participate in God's vision for the world's renewal. The event of sharing this good news of Jesus can bring about friendships and partnerships with non-Christians, and the process of building friendships and partnerships can lead to the event of evangelism. As we prayerfully share our lives and the good news with our friends, neighbors and colleagues, the Holy Spirit helps us to appreciate both the urgency to share the good news and the patience to love and cooperate with unbelievers.

When we limit evangelism to either process or event, things get messy. Some of us limit evangelism to the process of building friendships and collaborating with non-Christians without ever saying anything about Jesus. Refusing to share the good news is not-so-Christlike. It's also not very friendly, because eternity hangs in the balance. Friendship and collaboration with non-Christians is very Christlike, but if we don't speak of Jesus it's not evangelism.

Briefly, the work of Jesus in his life, death and resurrection is the defining moment in the story of God's pursuit of a sinful and rebellious world. With sin and evil ravaging humankind and the world, God sought to counteract evil first through the nation of Israel and ultimately through Jesus. God sent Jesus Christ his Son into the world to undo human and demonic evil through his life, ministry, death and resurrection. In his life and ministry, Jesus successfully overcame both temptation and the demonic forces of the world to emerge virtuous, the perfect example of true humanity. In his death, Jesus took upon himself the divine judgment that was due humankind for evil. In his resurrection, Jesus was raised by God his Father to a new kind of life, one that is eternally victorious over the forces of sin and death. On the Day of Judgment, Jesus will return to raise both those who believe in him and the entire created world to the same sin-free, death-free life. On that same day, all who have rejected the good news of Jesus will endure divine judgment. Admittedly it is hard to cover every facet of the gospel, but we can sum it up like this: In Jesus' life, death and resurrection God saves us from our slavery to sin in this life and eternal judgment in the next life.

Others limit evangelism to the event of sharing the gospel of Jesus with non-Christians. For these folks, the joys, needs, wisdom, passions and personalities of non-Christians aren't important. What's important is seeing souls saved for Jesus—HALLELUJAH!!! But the "soul" that needs salvation may have much to teach us about environmental activism, may need a ride to work, may be passionate about bird-watching or may just want to grab some Thai food with you—Hallelujah! All of these things are deeply important to God because God loves all of who we are, body and soul. We dare not ignore these things just so we can vomit the gospel all over someone's soul. That's just rude. And, if you hadn't guessed, not so Christlike.

In evangelism, we live with a paradox of urgency and patience. We urgently want people to come to know Jesus be-

cause of the new creation work that God longs to do in peoples' lives and in the world. Urgency is also necessary because
those who live apart from Jesus can die apart from him. This
leaves them under divine judgment when Jesus returns.

However, we must also exert patience in evangelism. God
himself patiently woos people through the Holy Spirit and
Christian witness. For many, conversion to Jesus is a journey
that may take years. If God has allotted this time to people,
then we ought to make sure we're in the flow of this process.

At times in our evangelism, urgency is called for. At other
times, loving patience is needed. In any case, all conversions
to Jesus are a result of divine urgency and divine patience.

SHARED BURDEN = EASY BURDEN

Jesus sends his disciples on their second evangelistic mission
two by two, speaking plainly about the risks: "Go your way;
behold, I send you out as lambs among wolves" (Luke 10:3
NKJV). Community is necessary in evangelism because evangelism is the most unnatural thing our Lord commands (yes, *commands*) us to do. For some of us evangelism is more unnatural
than prayer, fasting, living simply, sacrificial giving and doing
life together.[1] Christian community cuts through fear in evangelism, because our partnership in the gospel is itself a reminder
that Jesus is with us. Besides, it's a big relief to look in someone else's eyes and to see that he is just as sweaty with fear as
you are! And when you can be sweaty and fearful in front of
someone else, doesn't that speak to how close you've gotten?

Throughout his ministry, Jesus was encouraged and empowered by the divine community he had. The Holy Spirit em-

---

[1]Okay, sacrificial giving and Christ-centered community are pretty unnatural
too. They tie for second place.

powered Jesus for ministry (Matthew 3:16-17; 12:28; Luke 4:14). Jesus relied on the Spirit to enable his disciples to better understand his teachings after his departure (John 14:25-26; 16:13-15). Jesus also trusted that the Spirit would continue his work of convicting the world of its evil (John 16:7-11). The voice of God the Father confirmed both God's love for Jesus the Son (Matthew 3:17; Mark 9:7) and the truth of Jesus' own teaching (John 12:27-33).

Jesus also relied on his community of disciples throughout his ministry. Jesus' first disciples came from John the Baptist's crew (John 1:35-46). Jesus relied on his disciples for evangelistic networks (Mark 2:13-15). He trusted them to faithfully extend the reach of his own ministry during his life (Mark 3:14; Luke 9:1-6; 10:1-24) and after his resurrection and return to God his Father (John 14:12; Matthew 28:16-20). Jesus longed for his disciples' prayers and company before facing the crucifixion (Mark 14:32-42).

In light of Jesus' experience, we can say that God intends for mission and evangelism to be undertaken by communities of his people. There are several ways in which small groups can work together to see people come to know Jesus. Networking, praying together, launching Bible studies organized around an evangelistic investigation of God (InterVarsity calls them Groups Investigating God, or GIGs), encouraging and admonishing one another and exercising the gifts of the Spirit all play a role in seeing people come to faith.

NETWORKING

We often miss out on the power of networks in evangelism. We can tap into the gifts, talents, perspectives and resources of the whole body of Christ for the sake of reaching our friends with the gospel. Jabari, a leader in our ministry and a member in my small group, had asked me to speak with his friend Shemeka, a non-Christian with many questions and opinions about faith, the Bible and Jesus. Jabari needed help fielding some of her questions. When the three of us got together, laughter, disagreements, Bible verses and life-stories flowed freely. Over time Shemeka began to attend church with Jabari and me, and she developed friendships with other church members. One Sunday, when I was out of town at a conference, I got a call from my pastor: *Shemeka had committed her life to Jesus in the middle of the church service!* God brought about Shemeka's salvation through the collective efforts of Jabari and our church community.

Working together in this way gives non-Christians a sneak preview of the kind of community they will be part of when they choose to follow Jesus, and the pressure is off of us to be anything and everything to non-Christians. We can lean on the strength of our community, the body of Christ. The apostle Paul acknowledged his partnership with Apollos and with God in the conversion of the Christians at Corinth: "I planted, Apollos watered, but God gave the growth. So neither the one who plants nor the one who waters is anything, but only God who gives the growth" (1 Corinthians 3:6-7 NRSV). In many ways there's a communal energy involved in ushering someone into life with Jesus.

PRAYER

Though he resisted all of my invitations to come to know Jesus, Abe and I remained good friends throughout college. One day on my way to a small group I found Abe hunched over and weeping. The prognosis had leveled him: His grandmother's respiratory infection had overtaken her, and the doctors said she did not have long to live. Knowing this was the day I attended small group, Abe asked me if we would pray for his grandmother. "Of course we will," I said. Though I didn't feel the faith or confidence we religious types are supposed to summon up in times like these, our small group that day prayed for God's hand of healing on Abe's grandmother.

The next day Abe was all smiles and joy. With childlike glee he told me that his grandmother had made a recovery so remarkable that her doctors would be discharging her from the hospital the next week. "The doctors called it a miracle," he said. While Abe gently dismissed the notion that Jesus' hand was in this, he was grateful to know that I could be his go-to guy for prayer.

God worked through our small group's prayers to care for Abe's grandmother miraculously! We have a responsibility before our Father to intercede for our non-Christian friends in prayer. It's easy to pray solely for the salvation of our friends while we neglect to pray about their joys, passions, worries and day-to-day needs. God doesn't wait to care about all these things for us until we start following Jesus. He always cares about these things because they make us the persons we are, whether we are his children or not (Matthew 5:45; Acts 14:17). Without question, we must pray for the salvation of our friends because eternity is on the line. But many people come to know Jesus because they see God's work in the mundane, ordinary flow of life. God's work through our prayers can lead to a re-enchantment of day-to-day existence that points people to both God's love and their need for salvation through Jesus.

ENCOURAGEMENT, ADMONITION AND REJOICING

Because of the spectrum of responses to the good news of Jesus, our small group communities must be places of encouragement, admonition and rejoicing for people doing evangelism. This is nothing new, because all Christian communities ought to encourage, admonish and rejoice with one another. Our relationships are characterized by joy, fear, hostility, triumph, confusion and a plethora of other emotions. The good news of Jesus can usher in or challenge any of these emotions. Jesus' miracles, teachings and lifestyle made some folks (even dead people!) sing and shout. Other folks were deeply threatened by these things, and that caused friction between them and Jesus. Some of the same people saying, "Jesus is the King!" on Palm Sunday were saying "Crucify him!" on Good Friday. The good news giveth, and the good news taketh away.

Christians who share their faith need encouragement from their small groups because sharing the good news can be daunting. Sometimes we encounter hostility from non-Christians. At other times, our wonderful conversations with non-Christians may still result in our friends' unwillingness to give their lives to Jesus. In other instances, there's so much relational or cultural static between us and our friends that we can't figure out what in the world the Lord is (or is not) doing. Mutual encouragement in evangelism can give us a God's-eye view on our witnessing efforts. Hostile or apathetic responses to the good news can indicate that we are actually sharing the good news with integrity. The confusion that ensues as we share the good news can point to conceptual or cultural barriers that we have not accounted for. Mutual encouragement helps us to interpret the ways in which God is at work both in us and in the lives of non-Christian friends as we share our lives and the gospel with them.

We must also admonish one another in evangelism. Many non-Christians are rightly offended by our hypocrisy, false friendship and un-Christlike attitudes. We must truthfully confront one another when our lives betray Jesus' example. A former college instructor of mine, Elliot, once told me, "Myron, sometimes when we were talking about religious stuff, you were a loud-mouthed, rude jerk." She was the first person I ever had the privilege of leading to Jesus. Her words of admonition (she did some serious kung-fu on my ego) opened my eyes to ways that I had failed her in my witness and helped me to be a better witness to Jesus.

Small groups must rejoice over the work of God in evangelism. From the person who invited someone to church to the person who finally got the courage to bring Jesus up in a conversation, we must celebrate every step of faith in evangelism. Though our ultimate joy is found in the conversion of our friends, we can celebrate everything along the way because our labors for the sake of the gospel are never in vain. At the very least, we should celebrate God's work in our lives as we strive for the gospel. And even if we don't have the privilege of leading a friend to Jesus, we may have laid a foundation that someone else can build on. This, too, is worthy of celebration. So sweat the small triumphs. Rejoice your head off.

GROUPS INVESTIGATING GOD

When Avery informed our small group that he had been discussing Jesus with a non-Christian grad student named Billy, I was glad to give him some GIG guides to give their conversations more concrete direction about Jesus and faith. Billy accepted Avery's invitation to do a GIG, and our group regularly prayed for them, with Avery giving the group updates on God's work in their friendship. Avery extended the reach of his friendship by connecting Billy with other small group members. Billy even attended some church services with Avery and other small group members. Ultimately, Billy placed his faith in Jesus, and he and Avery would go on to lead Billy's fiancée to faith in

Jesus as well. By simply supplying Avery with resources, praying and following Avery's lead into friendship with Billy, our community affirmed Avery's evangelistic work.[2]

SPIRITUAL GIFTS

Our spiritual gifts can be powerful on-ramps to evangelism. If the Lord Jesus has given spiritual gifts to all believers through the power of the Holy Spirit (Ephesians 4:7-13; 1 Corinthians 12; 14), then we can rest assured that small groups have a diversity of spiritual gifts at their disposal to accomplish the work of God.

In his book *Reimagining Evangelism*, Rick Richardson identifies seven key gift areas that powerfully equip and enable Christian communities for evangelism: (1) organizing and leading (Romans 12:8; 1 Corinthians 12:28); (2) evangelism and equipping (Ephesians 4:11); (3) hospitality and encouragement (Romans 12:8-13); (4) pastoring and teaching (Romans 12:7; 1 Corinthians 12:29; Ephesians 4:11); (5) prayer, words and works from the Holy Spirit (1 Corinthians 12:7-10, 28-31; Romans 12:6; Ephesians 4:11); (6) service and mercy (Romans 12:7-8; 1 Corinthians 12:28); (7) giving (Romans 12:8).[3] Though some of us are still in the process of discerning what our spiritual gifts are, all followers of Jesus have them. In reference to evangelism, two questions are set before all of us:

How will we implement our gifts to equip our Christian community to reach out to non-Christians?

How will we implement our gifts to touch the lives of nonbelievers?

---

[2]See the appendix for more resources.
[3]Rick Richardson, *Reimagining Evangelism* (Downers Grove, Ill.: InterVarsity Press, 2006), pp. 55-63. Richardson's book is one of the best books I've ever read on evangelism. Run out and get a copy ASAP!

My small group at the University of New Orleans employed the spiritual gifts of its members to reach out to non-Christians on a regular basis. In the course of a year, we saw a handful of people come to know Jesus as small group members organized parties (hospitality, administration); spoke well-timed, Spirit-inspired words to people (words from the Holy Spirit); and ministered to people in times of deep need (mercy). The hospitality and administration created safe spaces were Christians and non-Christians could be together and simply enjoy one another's company. The wisdom believers spoke into people's lives demonstrated God's care for what some considered the "non-spiritual" parts of their lives. The acts of mercy ranged from simple things like helping people out with their homework to walking with them in the midst of emotional distress. Granted, at different points the good news of Jesus had to be shared and explained, but the fleshing out of the good news through the use of these gifts was invaluable.

Networking, praying together, launching GIGs, encouraging and admonishing one another and the exercise of the gifts of the Spirit afford small groups the opportunity to work together in evangelism. Through these activities, all the members of the body of Christ are invited to follow Jesus in the power of the Spirit in bringing the gospel to bear on the lives of non-Christians.

OUR LORD WALKS WITH US

The cross at the center of the Christian faith is a constant reminder of God's love for the world. The same cross is also a testament to the world's hostility toward God and God's people. While the reality of the world's hostility can cause us to shrink back from Jesus' mandate to share the good news, we must bear in mind that Jesus is "gentle and humble in heart";

the yoke of his commands are easy and his burden is light (Matthew 11:28-30). In evangelism, as in all things, it is Jesus who does the heavy lifting. It is in and through Spirit-filled Christian communities that he shoulders the load. The power of Jesus manifested through his people is a source of strength and comfort as he sends us out into a chaotic, broken world. When Jesus works through us to bring people from darkness into his light, we have more proof that he truly has overcome evil. As you and your small group shine like stars in the darkness may you joyfully discover that Jesus' commandment is not a burden at all.

9

SMALL GROUP MISSION

Sandra Van Opstal

I AM A STORY JUNKIE. I enjoy hearing them, and I enjoy telling them. When I watch movies I get sucked into the story and act as if I am in it. I talk back to the TV, and sometimes when a scene gets too intense, I get up and leave the room.

The New Testament is that kind of intense story for me. This marginalized small group of just over a hundred people became a worldwide force! Sometimes I feel like taking a time out from the gripping and provocative story about God's mission that unfolds in the Bible, but I keep coming back because it helps me understand our legacy as Christians.

Mission—at least in the context of discussing small groups—is a broad word describing God's work reconciling nations, genders, races, socioeconomic groups, neighborhoods and even the created order.

For God was pleased to have all his fullness dwell in him (Christ), and through him to reconcile to himself all things, whether things on earth or things in heaven, by making peace through his blood, shed on the cross. (Colossians 1:19-20)

The act of participating in God's mission involves leaning into the reality that God is already at work, bringing healing and victory to replace brokenness and defeat. As God's people, we are called not only to be reconciled ourselves to God but to be a part of his work of restoration and reconciliation in the world. This is what it means to participate in God's mission, and as we engage in it we are finding our true work in the world as Christ's ambassadors.

A GOOD STORY

As a young child I was aware that the world we lived in was messy. I could tell things just weren't right. At eight years old I could not find a Barbie that looked anything like me or my darker-hued friends. I was so upset that I wrote Mattel a letter explaining the need for dolls that represent the diversity of the world. I argued that my friends and I needed to have brown Barbies with black hair. It was as compelling a letter as an eight-year-old could write, but it was clear to me that I was being overlooked. This may seem like a minor incident, but the experience of my community being overlooked is ongoing: I was and am an "outsider" in my culture.

How did you become aware of the mess in the world? Maybe you knew about it growing up. Maybe you took a class in college, went on a global or urban missions project, or just read the news. When we see the state of our broken world, our hearts should cry out, "Somebody has got to do something about this mess!"

That statement begs the question, just who is "somebody"?

Most of us know the command to "love the LORD your God with all your heart and with all your soul and with all your strength" and "love your neighbor as yourself" (Deuteronomy 6:5; Leviticus 19:18). However, many of us are more comfortable with the intellectual exercise offered by the theologian in Luke 10:29 "Who is my neighbor?" than we are with the practical exercise of loving those around us, whoever they are.

Jesus responded to this question with a story: An Israelite man gets brutally mugged on the road. Immediately, we think, *somebody's got to do something about this mess!* Three fellow Israelites see the messed-up man and pass by on the other side of the road. Jesus' audience understood "neighbor" to mean "fellow Israelite," so already, a scandal is apparent: the "somebodys" who ought to care are going out of their way to avoid seeing or doing anything. Suddenly, along comes a Samaritan man, whose race and culture was summarily despised by the Israelites, and he becomes the "somebody"—the neighbor who sees, cares and acts!

This story was offensive to its hearers because it was casting their enemy as the model of love. It is a picture of restoration—the mugged man is made whole thanks to the intervention of the Samaritan—but the story also points to the larger theme of reconciliation. The new news from Jesus is as scandalous as the Israelites' inaction: The lesson is not so much that you have to love your neighbor as yourself—that much is evident from the Hebrew Scriptures—but that *who* your neighbor is goes beyond race, culture or socioeconomic status. God's people see, care and act!

Many things cause us to "pass by" when we encounter suffering or messed-up parts of our world. Many of us have little to no contact with our neighbors. This may be due to social rules and conventions; maybe also we live in places that keep the mess out of sight. We're content with culture-bound moralizing about the achievement of success, content to remain ignorant of the real challenges faced by others. Circumstances like these become the rules we follow; they tell us how we "should" engage—or not—with our neighbors.

We need each other to help us have the courage to see and act on the things we don't want to see. Small groups can be a place where missional Christians help each other reflect the kingdom—to see the things we don't want to see, to care and to act.

BREAKING THE RULES

I remember when my small group began to break the rules. We had been doing a study for weeks; the application point was "In what ways is God using you to proclaim "good news" for the captives?" We had a wonderful discussion around the concept but missed getting to action. One of our small group members had been doing a counseling internship; she asked us if we would be interested in hosting a baby shower for single moms. These were moms who did not have the financial ability to purchase the things their child needed. Even more important, these moms hadn't had anyone celebrate their coming child. Who celebrates inappropriate behaviors, after all?

We all were excited about the chance to celebrate these women as "neighbors." Our leader reached out to other small groups in the church to see if they wanted to participate by purchasing gifts or donating money. One group worked on the decorations and another on the food. There was a buzz about what we were doing, and the party was a success! The young mothers had their physical needs met, yes, but the delight in the eyes of the women who were being celebrated clearly communicated that they felt cared for as well.

One of our group members, a young Korean who had recently graduated from college, had never been to a baby shower. Playing baby food games and celebrating the coming births of children to black and Latino single moms was an experience I imagine he'll never forget. His presence there defied racial, socioeconomic and gender boundaries and still leads me to tears. I imagine it was an experience he will never forget.

We had practiced compassion as a small group before, but that event was a turning point for us. We enjoyed building into our community, we worked toward a goal together, we prayed for the event and the moms afterward and we saw individual growth for each person.

Parties for unwed mothers, rallies for affordable housing, confessing to people of other races about our own racism and inviting their correction. What can your small group do to break the rules? What distracts you from seeing and responding to the mess God wants us to do something about? Remember, *somebody's got to do something about this mess!*

SEEING, CARING, ACTING

One thing your group can commit to is to be informed. Some small groups pray in response to the weekly news, becoming conscious of the troubles of the day and making the connection between the group, the problem and God. Other small groups take classes together that address particular challenges to their community or world. Some groups capitalize on the passions and connections of individual members in order to inform the entire community. Still others choose to see movies together that will expand their understanding of complex social problems.

The most important challenge is not to merely see but to grow our hearts. This means connecting to real people, intentionally placing ourselves in a position to hear stories. Where does your small group dine or hang out? Where do you volunteer together where you are going to be with people different from you? As a small group leader you can look for opportunities to expand your group members' comfort zones.

It's not enough, of course, to see and care. God's people also act. We need to speak out and fight against injustice where it is happening, whether it is on our block or twenty miles west of us. As a small group we can write government officials and speak out when policies that affect the under-resourced are being voted on. We can also hold one another to living simply so that we can use our resources to provide for others. Small groups might invite the homeless to eat with them and share their stories. Small groups might collect and distribute computers to people with less access, and build relationships while teaching them how to use them. Small groups might take their "neighborhood" on the road to address pressing needs in other communities through disaster relief or short-term service projects.

Imagine if your small group embodied reconciliation beyond cultural, racial and socioeconomic boundaries. What if people outside your group saw you as neighbors who took on tough challenges in the neighborhood and consistently showed mercy and compassion to those who needed it? Maybe your head is spinning. Maybe you feel lost as to your next steps. Here are some ideas for what action you can take to lead your small group into a missional way of living.

PARTNERING WITH OTHER GROUPS

One outlet for small group mission is to partner with a group that has a *similar identity.* La Fe, the Latino Bible study at Northwestern University, partnered with Alianza, the Latino student group on campus, to host an evangelistic event on Dia de Los Muertos ("Day of the Dead") to invite Latinos to think about the spiritual journey of their community. We also sent a group of people to a march for immigration reform held in Chicago. It was a great way to utilize a common identity and values for mission. It opened doors to further partnership in compassion and advocacy, as well as providing evangelistic opportunities.

Another idea for collaboration is with groups that have a *similar goal* in mind. That could be any justice work from advocacy for refugees to affordable housing. One small group has considered what they might do to live the gospel in their suburb where affordable housing is a crucial issue. They have worked alongside community organizations that appeal to the town council and mayor so that new developments keep low-income families in mind. Another small group in a small rural town works alongside a relief agency to ensure that displaced families from war-torn countries are aware of their rights.

Partnerships with nonfaith-based groups can be especially enriching for a small group to participate in. Imagine a men's group that, instead of camping, takes their annual trip with a restoration project in an area devastated by a natural disaster. This provides the group an opportunity to bond as a community, live out compassion and be witnesses to the folks on their work site who do not yet know Jesus.

Some of the best evangelistic conversations I had in college happened on a similar trip. A portion of our small group did not want to do a traditional "spring break" trip, so we all went to work on flood relief with Habitat for Humanity. Every night while debriefing our work day we shared stories and talked about life values and goals. At the end of the trip two of the people made significant steps in their faith journey. That experience gave me a picture of how small groups could experience community and mission (both evangelism and compassion) at once.

As small groups work in partnership with other organizations, it is important for them to keep their identity as a transformational community, but part of being transformed is learning to see, care and act on behalf of our neighbors. Often that leads us outside of the traditional boundaries of Christian fellowship and into the world that God created.

TRANSFORMED BY MISSION

What would it be like if each of our small groups was actively involved in mission? How would we be different as individuals and as a community? Luke gives us a picture of what that might look like in the book of Acts.

In Acts 10 we find Peter, a Jew who has grown up with a huge cultural bias against Gentiles, having a strange dream. God calls him to enter the house of a Gentile and eat with him. This is scandalous—even more so than Jesus' story of the Good Samaritan! But it is clear to Peter that God is calling him to do it. In the face of such a scary challenge, Peter takes his small group with him, for courage and collaboration. God does something amazing, even absurd—Gentiles are brought to know Christ!

After seeing what God has done, Peter knows that this radical transformation will be thought absurd and even offensive to the church. He is concerned that the rest of the church get on board with him in opening the gospel to the Gentiles. So in Acts 11 we see him go to the church leaders, where their initial response is "How dare you? You're nuts!"

Peter has anticipated this reaction. He retells the story "precisely as it had happened" (verse 4), and he brings along his small group—"these six brothers" (verse 12) who had experienced this with him—to corroborate his story and help the church leaders understand. Peter remains committed to both communities—the old, Jewish one and the new, Gentile one—and to bringing them together. He doesn't give up on them but instead continues to build relationship with both sides of his community until they all understand God's call. But he doesn't do it alone; he knows how vital his small group is to this process. And not just his small group or even the church in Jerusalem but the whole history of the church was changed by his experience.

We're not just called to personal mission; we're called to be a transformative community, and that involves influencing others to mission. God calls us to life transformation, not just one-time experience, and he calls us to engage and embrace our communities as part of that transformation. So when God calls us into an experience, we are also called to help others to understand how God showed up among us. We often do this most effectively in community.

As Peter and his team experienced, a small group that prepares together, goes together and comes back together experiences the kind of transformation that God intends for his people. They become better equipped to see, care and act together—and they become a witness to God's reconciling, restorative mission for the world. That's a story worth hearing, a story worth living.

10

PASSING THE BATON

IDENTIFYING AND DEVELOPING LEADERS

Jay Anderson

ALL CALVIN SMITH had to do was get the baton to Lee McNeill.

Carl Lewis waited breathlessly as he watched his team-mates competing in the preliminary heat of the Men's 4 x 100 meter relays in the 1988 Summer Olympic Games in Seoul, South Korea. The United States track and field team was ex-pected to win seven gold medals that summer, including one in the 4 x 100 relay.

Lewis anchored the 4 x 100 team. He was hoping to recap-ture the four gold medals he had won in the Los Angeles Sum-mer Olympics in 1984. He and Ben Johnson of Canada had battled back and forth for several years for the unofficial title of "The World's Fastest Man," dueling in the 100-meter sprints on many occasions. Their match-up in the finals of that event during the Olympics was much anticipated. The outcome of the 4 x 100 relay, on the other hand, was pretty much a foregone conclusion. The U.S. team was expected to win the gold, and win easily.

Lewis was held out of the preliminaries for the event, so as to be fresh for the finals and for the other events he was competing in. Each of the four U.S. runners in the qualifying heat—Dennis Mitchell, Albert Robinson, Calvin Smith and Lee McNeill—would run one hundred meters, the first three passing a baton to a teammate at the end of their leg of the race. The last runner just had to receive the baton and dash to the finish line. Mitchell, Robinson, Smith and McNeill were each extremely talented sprinters in their own right, and easily the fastest team in their qualifying heat. There was little doubt about them advancing into the finals.

As expected, the beginning of the race went very well for the U.S. team. They built a sizable lead, and it appeared that they were going to be able to coast to the finish line. However, just before the last leg of the race, Calvin Smith bobbled the baton pass to Lee McNeill. By the time they had successfully executed the handing off of the baton, they were outside the designated zone and were disqualified. Carl Lewis, the world's fastest man, never got a chance to run for his gold medal in the 4 x 100 relays.[1]

One of the most important things you can do as a leader is pass along the training you have received to another (potential) leader. If you fail to pass along the skills and training you have received, someone else might miss out on the opportunity to show what they can do as a small group leader. More important, if you fail to multiply yourself as a leader—or at the very least replace yourself—the mission of

---

[1]For the full story, see Kenny Moore, "Man, Not Superman," *Sports Illustrated,* accessed September 29, 2009, at <http://sportsillustrated.cnn.com/vault/article/magazine/MAG1067848/index.htm>.

your InterVarsity chapter or your congregation, and the larger mission of the church as a whole, suffers a significant setback.

Jesus said, "The harvest is plentiful, but the workers are few. Ask the Lord of the harvest, therefore, to send out workers into his harvest field" (Matthew 9:37-38). There will probably never be enough laborers for the harvest in the kingdom; in fact, in my experience with InterVarsity Christian Fellowship, the number of capable, trained small group leaders is often the key limiting factor in the size and strength of a chapter. With students graduating and moving on in regular intervals, any InterVarsity chapter is only four years away from extinction. If small group leaders don't replace themselves by the time they graduate, there is a great likelihood that the chapter will decrease in size.

So at a bare minimum you should work toward replacing yourself as a small group leader. But it's better to *multiply yourself.* A good friend of mine, Mike Bottrell, is fond of an image that teaches the power of spiritual multiplication in disciple-making. I think it is just as applicable to the multiplication of small group leaders. If you, over the course of ten years as a leader, were to just lead your group and never invest in future leaders, the number of small group leaders would remain constant: one! But, if each year you invested in a potential leader, and by the end of the year, trained and equipped and encouraged *them* to be a leader, and then sent them off to lead a small group of their own, in ten years, the number of small group leaders will have grown to eleven: you plus the ten leaders you trained.

Not bad, but here's where the boring math lesson gets exciting: If you were to develop one small group leader each year for ten years, and ensure that each of those small group leaders developed leaders themselves, who would in turn develop other leaders, at the end of ten years there would be over a thousand small group leaders. That's a lot of laborers for the harvest!

I will grant that you will probably never be able to achieve a 100 percent success rate for leadership multiplication. You may not be able to find a new leader every year, and not every leader will be able to turn right around and develop a new, multiplying leader in a year, despite your best efforts. But the principle still is noteworthy. If we want our ministries to grow, if we want the kingdom to expand, if we want more people to experience the community and Bible study and missional outreach that we have described in this book, we need to think multiplicatively.

I hope to lay out in this chapter a relatively simple process toward that end. The first step is to recognize potential leaders that are in your group. The second step is to begin intentionally investing in them. The next step is to develop them as leaders—training them and encouraging them for the role of small group leader. And the final step is to invite them into a leadership role.

RECOGNIZING POTENTIAL LEADERS

There are any number of combinations of different personality types and leadership gifts that can lead to a person's success as a small group leader. The first InterVarsity small group I ever participated in was led by someone who, at first glance, may not have struck you as an outstanding leader. Dan was soft-spoken and somewhat shy—certainly not the life of the party. But he was a solid Christian, with a love for God's Word and a heart for other people. He was always exceptionally well prepared for Bible study: not only did he always know the passage extremely well, but he also usually did some extra research to discover historical or cultural background information that helped us to understand the text and its meaning.

On the other end of the introvert-extrovert spectrum was my friend Bob. He and I co-led a study our senior year at the Milwaukee School of Engineering. Bob was still relatively young in his faith at the time, but what he lacked in spiritual maturity and Bible study leading experience, he more than made up for with enthusiasm and creativity. We could always count on Bob for a zany community-building activity or a unique way of driving home the application point of the passage. Bob *was* the life of the party, and our study grew to about twenty members in large part because of Bob's charisma (and the great food he always made sure we had on hand)! We eventually had to divide the group into three to ensure that everyone got to participate meaningfully in discussion. One of those groups was led by Dan, who helped provide depth and richness to our study with his thorough preparation.

Another great Bible study leader, Cathy, was like Dan always well-prepared, but what made her stand out as a leader was her personal warmth and friendliness. She would always ask you how you were doing, and you could tell that she actually cared about your answer to her question. She made everyone feel welcome and accepted and affirmed. Her strongest suit was her care and compassion. She genuinely cared about everyone in her group.

There is no one "right" way to be a small group leader. God will be able to take your own unique mix of personality, temperament and spiritual gifts to benefit your small group. And he can use someone very different from you to effectively lead another group. Don't get locked into thinking a small group leader fits a certain profile. God can use all different kinds of people to be small group leaders.

So, if there is no one particular personality type or spiritual gift to look for, how will I know a potential leader when I see one? Great question! The first answer is to pray and ask for discernment. Jesus spent extended time in prayer before he picked the twelve disciples that he was going to designate as apostles. In fact, Luke tells us that he spent the entire night in prayer (Luke 6:12)! If Jesus needed to pray all night before picking the future leaders he was going to invest in, then we probably should pray as well!

After praying, let me suggest you look for "FAT" people to lead your groups. No, that is not a discriminatory comment against people who are thin. "FAT" is an old InterVarsity acronym for Faithful, Available and Teachable.

Consistency should be a high value as you look for new leaders, but we use the term *faithful* because no one wants to be led by CAT people. (Take that, cat lovers!) Faithful people are at small group every week; if they can't make it, they call (apologetically!) in advance to let you know. They are dependable and trustworthy. If you ask them to do something, they'll take care of it and then ask if there is anything else they can do to be of help.

Being *available* is a challenge when there's always more than one thing vying for people's attention. We live in a hyperscheduled, overactive society. People's commitment level to any one thing is often lower as a result. A student who is involved in seven other organizations (serving as an officer in four of them) and three intramural teams, working thirty hours a week and volunteering every weekend at a homeless shelter is probably not "available" to take on the significant spiritual responsibility of being a small group leader. Their busyness doesn't necessarily disqualify them from leadership, but it may suggest that you would have to ask them to consider dropping out of a few activities in order to add being a small group leader to their schedule. Available people are able and willing to make a small group—and the people in it—a priority in their schedule.

You don't want to ask an arrogant know-it-all to lead a study. Rather, you want someone *teachable*. Though the flashy, outspoken life-of-the-party person in your small group might have a lot of charisma, they might not be ready spiritually to serve. "God opposes the proud but gives grace to the humble" (James 4:6). Small groups require humble, teachable, servant-hearted leaders.

I don't want give the impression that extroverted, outgoing people should be excluded from leadership. Outgoing people are often outstanding leaders. So, besides FAT people, you should also be on the lookout for SCRAPPy people.

"SCRAPPy" people are Socially Confident, Relationally Adept and Potentially Prideful. These people may have a few rough edges that need to be addressed, but they can be key gatherers for a group. Their natural winsomeness and charisma can serve as a magnet to attract others. We can't turn a blind eye to people who are unrepentant about sin in their lives, but investing in a FAT SCRAPPy person can pay great dividends.

I served on staff with InterVarsity for several years at the University of Wisconsin–River Falls. When I inherited the chapter, it was really struggling. Our large group meetings were hardly "large"—being attended by only a handful of regulars—and we had no small group network to speak of. Along came a SCRAPPy little freshman guy, Greg. Was he faithful? Not always. Was he available? Not entirely. Was he teachable? Not all the time. But was he a great leader? Definitely.

Greg was just dripping with charisma. It seemed that everyone on campus knew him and that everyone who knew him liked him. He was very bold—almost fearless—about inviting people to our meetings. Soon he was asked to become the master of ceremonies (and life of the party!) for our now-growing large group meetings. By the time he graduated, our small, struggling chapter of twelve to fifteen had grown to over seventy-five. God used Greg (together with a cadre of FAT people) to grow the River Falls chapter to a size and strength it still has today—fifteen years later. By all means, invest in FAT people, but don't overlook the SCRAPPy ones!

INTENTIONALLY INVESTING IN POTENTIAL LEADERS

Once you have identified potential leaders, the next step in passing the baton is to begin intentionally investing in them. Just as there is no one right way to be a small group leader, there is no "one-size-fits-all" approach to leadership development. Since every potential leader is different, each will require a unique investment of time and energy in order to best develop and grow as a leader.

Sometimes it is hard to know what exactly they need in order to grow. To a certain extent, you need to be like a gardener planting a new plant in their garden. Most plants need good soil, adequate water and the right amount of sunlight. Some plants, however, like a thick, rich soil; others prefer a thinner, sandier soil. Some plants require a lot of moisture and need to be watered often; if you forget to water them, they droop or even lose their leaves entirely. Other plants actually bloom best if under-watered. Some plants love full sunlight and bright sun—I have some flowers that make magnificent blooms when I plant them in a sunny location. In a shadier location, they hardly bloom at all. Optimal plant growth occurs when you remember the essential elements—

water, sunlight, good soil—but tailor the mix of elements to the particular needs of each plant. Similarly, you will need to experiment a bit to figure out what combination of things works best with each person to cause them to grow. But it will probably be some combination of three key things: time, affirmation and opportunity.

Time is probably the most important thing you can offer an up-and-coming leader in your group. It is noteworthy that Jesus spent three whole years with his disciples preparing them to carry on the ministry he started. He spent nearly every waking moment with his disciples over the course of those three years—eating together, traveling together, working together, ministering together.

Before you panic and think *I don't have much time to invest!* let me reassure you that I'm not actually suggesting that you add a whole lot to your schedule. Instead, do the things that you are already doing; just do them *with* your leader-in-training. Make teachable moments along the way to guide and to instruct and model. Eat some meals together. Go to the library together. Go on road trips to conferences or spring break mission trips together. Any shared experience is an opportunity to build trust and community, as well as an opportunity for a teachable moment. That's a lot of what we have recorded for us in the Gospels. Jesus is hanging out with the disciples or doing some ministry or just traveling from town to town. Then, in the course of their normal, ordinary daily routine and activities, he offers a timely word of affirmation or rebuke, and the disciples never forget it. They are changed forever by a few simple words, spoken at just the right time, during a teachable moment. To get those moments, you have to be together. So plan to invest some time in your future leader.

As you spend time with them, you will begin to notice some

of their passions or interests or inclinations or, perhaps, spiritual gifts. For instance, you may notice that when Joe talks, people really listen; he always seems to give sound advice and have deep insight into the Scripture your group is studying. When Emma says, "Let's go to a movie!" everyone says yes. When Sarah arranges a social activity, not many show up, but when she prays, stuff happens—it's almost uncanny how often her prayers seem to get answered. Erik loves to cook and bake, and always seems to bring something good for your small group to eat. Mandy is kind of quiet but always sticks around after the party to wash the dishes and tidy up.

Mandy may have the spiritual gift of service, while Erik may have the gift of hospitality. Sarah may be gifted in intercession, and Joe might have the gifts of wisdom and discernment. I'm not sure what to call Emma's gift—"gathering" or "inviting"? Whatever you call it, it is invaluable to a small group, and I suspect it is one mode of the spiritual gift of leadership.

One of the most powerful things you can do as a leader is call out and affirm those gifts as you see them in your small group members. They may not even recognize the gifts or abilities themselves, and most often will not see how their gifts can contribute to the life and health of your small group. Apart from your initiative and affirmation, few will recognize themselves as a potential leader. Most will need to be affirmed in their gifts and abilities, and then shown how they could use those gifts and abilities to lead and to serve others. Then they will need to be invited into leadership and given encouragement that they can actually do it.

This is where the third ingredient—*opportunity*—comes into play. After you have recognized and affirmed a potential leader's unique gifts and abilities, you need to give them an opportunity to "try them on." Give someone who seems to have a heart for prayer the opportunity to lead the prayer section of your small group meeting time. Give a natural gatherer the opportunity to organize your small group's next social outing. Give the person who loves to bake and cook an official role: "Hospitality Coordinator." Help the individual who seems to have great insights into the Scriptures prepare to lead a session that you have to miss. Delegation is a great way to develop both ownership and future leadership.

People who feel like they have an important contribution to make to the small group are much more likely to be committed members, and people who successfully serve in small ways are much more likely later to be willing to take on more responsibilities. Jesus said, "Whoever can be trusted with very little can also be trusted with much" (Luke 16:10). In other words, if someone is faithful in small things, they may then be entrusted with bigger things later.

When I was just getting involved with the InterVarsity chapter at the Milwaukee School of Engineering, I was asked to bring the overhead projector to the large group meetings. I realize that this dates me a little bit; some people may not even know what an overhead projector is! Basically a forerunner to video projection, it allowed words written on a transparent piece of plastic to be projected onto a wall or screen. My job was to check out the overhead projector unit from the library each week, bring it to our large group meeting space and set it up.

Pretty simple, right? But it earned me the important sounding title of "Audio-Visual Technician," and it was one less thing that our large group coordinator had to take care of before the meeting started. Perhaps most importantly, it ensured that I would be at the large group meeting every week—which was probably the main reason I was asked me to do it. I was pretty serious about my homework, and without the job of AV Techie, I might have often skipped the meeting to study. But having a role in the meeting helped me feel more a part of the chapter and helped me see what was involved in pulling a gathering together every week, which helped prepare me for the following year, when I became large group coordinator—which in turn was great preparation for serving as chapter president the year after that, which proved to be invaluable training and preparation for later coming on staff with InterVarsity. And then, after a couple years on staff, I was asked to supervise several other staff in our area.

"He who can be trusted with little can also be trusted with much." You could say that my preparation to supervise eleven people working on five different campuses started the day I accepted the job of AV Techie my freshman year at the Milwaukee School of Engineering. You never know what path or trajectory of leadership you might launch people into by giving them a simple opportunity to serve!

LEADERSHIP DEVELOPMENT

Once a potential leader's gifts have been recognized and affirmed and called out, and once they have been invited to "try on" a leadership role, they need to be developed as leaders. Ephesians 4:12 says that it is the role of the leaders of a body of believers to "prepare [or equip] God's people for works of service, so that the body of Christ may be built up." For the body of Christ to be built up, we need to develop every member of the body of Christ that has been entrusted to us, but especially future leaders. A tried and true process for developing and training future leaders is to teach, demonstrate, observe, evaluate and encourage.

The first step in the training process is to *teach* the trainee the important information they need to know in order to succeed in the role. So as you think about training in an apprentice small group leader, you need to teach them about the things you have learned: how to lead inductive Bible study, how to prepare and lead a good discussion, how to build a sense of community and mobilize small group members for ministry. And, of course, you have to teach them the importance of identifying and developing future leaders.

Teaching is the first and most critical step in the training process. The second step is to *demonstrate*. Teach them the key elements of a small group, and then clearly model those elements in your next meeting. After you have given them some instruction in inductive Bible study, walk through the inductive method in a short, simple passage. Teach them the importance of community or outreach, and then demonstrate what that looks like by doing it in a real small group setting.

Now they are ready to give it a try on their own. The next step in the process is to *observe*. Let them try their hand at leading while you watch and observe. Of course, you want to do everything in your power to help ensure that they enjoy success during their first experience trying something new, but don't expect perfection. That's where the last two steps of the process come in: *evaluating* and *encouraging*.

Evaluation and encouragement work together. Without good, critical evaluation, a leader will likely persist in bad habits. But without encouragement, they might become disheartened and quit entirely. Good coaches tell you not only what you are doing right, but what you are doing wrong. They will encourage you to keep doing what is right, and tell you how to change what you did wrong to ensure better results the next time.

For the best results, evaluation and encouragement must be dispensed in the right "dosage." Most people tend to hear critique more strongly, so you probably need to find three to five (or more!) encouraging things to say for every suggestion or critique you offer. Some people welcome critique and feedback, seeing it as an opportunity to grow and improve. For them, you can dispense evaluation and encouragement in equal doses. Others are a little too confident in themselves and their abilities. They may need to hear quite a bit of negative feedback in order to recognize their limitations and see their need for improvement. Whatever the case, be sure to offer both evaluation *and* encouragement as they try their hand at leading.

Of course, being a small group leader is not just one skill. It is a combination of numerous skills. So you will likely have to repeat the training process several times as the potential leader you are working with adds new skills to their repertoire. And, so they don't get overwhelmed, let me suggest focusing in on just one or two things at a time. But this doesn't mean that the training process has to take forever. For instance, after teaching and demonstrating inductive Bible study and leading a discussion, you can spend a couple of weeks giving evaluation and encouragement on those subjects. But you can simultaneously move on to the next skill—developing community, for instance—and begin teaching and demonstrating the essentials of that topic.

The entire process—teaching, demonstrating, observing, evaluating and encouraging—is an ongoing cycle that you repeat numerous times in the course of training a leader. Over time, you won't even need to think about it, but you will begin to do it unconsciously as you develop others in leadership.

INVITING INTO LEADERSHIP

The final step in the process of passing the baton is to invite them to step into a leadership role. Even if you have successfully managed all the steps up until this point, if you fail to complete this last step, your race is in vain. Why? Simply put, most people do not see themselves as leaders and need to be encouraged to take on a spiritual leadership role. Most will not be bold enough to put themselves forward as a potential leader. More often than not, people don't see themselves as leaders, and, even if you can convince them they have what it takes to be a leader, they may still be reluctant to do so. Your job as a leader is to invite them and encourage them!

In some settings, small group leaders may not have the authority to invite new people into leadership. That responsibility and authority may be given to someone else—your ministry leadership team, a small groups pastor or your InterVarsity staffworker, for example. So before you proceed with this step, you should check with the person in authority over you. You need to work within the leadership selection process parameters of the ministry you are a part of.

At the University of Wisconsin–Eau Claire, where I am on staff with InterVarsity, we generally invite people into leadership toward the end of the spring semester, in mid-April or so. By then, we hope that our small group leaders have done all the prior work of identifying future leaders, intentionally investing in them and beginning to train them in the basics of small group leadership. In fact, we encourage people to identify an apprentice or two at the *start* of the spring semester, so that they have adequate time to invest in and train the future leaders in their group. Each potential leader is then personally invited by their group leader into the role for the fall. The invitation includes not just affirmation and encouragement but also a clear set of our chapter's expectations for small group leaders. We ask all our small group leaders to not only commit to the job description we have written up for small group leaders but also to sign on to the covenant that all of our leaders affirm and ascribe to. (See examples in the appendix.) That way, they know what they are getting into when they sign on for the role, and there are no unpleasant surprises later.

I have learned the hard way that you are much better off with fewer, highly committed small group leaders than a bunch of leaders who aren't very committed at all. Our criteria for leadership selection is the three Cs: committed to Christ, committed to the chapter and committed to the covenant.

If someone is very gifted and talented and has lots of charisma but is wavering in their faith, they should not be invited into leadership.

If someone is a solid, mature Christian with lots of gifts but is overly involved in other activities or academics or is bouncing between several ministries, they will probably not be effective as a leader. For them to bear fruit *in* the chapter, they must be committed *to* the chapter. They can be challenged to commit to just one group, or to place as much priority on ministry as they do their academics, but it doesn't serve anyone—the chapter, the small group or the potential small group leader—to have someone who is only half-committed to the role.

Finally, if a potential small group leader doesn't identify with the priorities included in a ministry's covenant, they're probably not an ideal candidate for a small group leader role. For example, the small group leader (as we've seen in this book) is critical in modeling and mobilizing outreach. A potential leader who is not interested in outreach might be better suited to serve in other ways. A person who doesn't feel competent or confident in outreach can get further training and encouragement, but if someone is unwilling to make outreach a priority, then it's best to find another, less critical role for them.

Once we have invited potential leaders to consider step-
ping into the small group leader role, and have clearly communicated our expectations, and have asked them to prayerfully make a decision about whether or not to lead, we have an
induction ceremony for those who have said yes. Our leadership induction ceremony at the University of Wisconsin–Eau
Claire includes a formal signing of a book that contains our
chapter covenant. By signing, future leaders are joining the
generations of previous leaders who have committed before
God and one another to carry on the vision of the chapter and
to pass it along to future generations. Then every new small
group leader is handed a wooden baton from the leader who
trained and invested in them and is charged with passing that
baton of leadership on to a successor.

To emphasize and reinforce the importance of raising up
future leaders, we inscribe the words of 2 Timothy 2:2 onto
the baton. The apostle Paul, as he was nearing the end of his
life, charged his young protégé Timothy with the responsibility of finding and identifying future leaders who would be
able to multiply their leadership: "The things you have heard
me say . . . entrust to reliable people who will also be quali-
fied to teach others." We charge our small group leaders
with the responsibility of identifying an apprentice, training
and developing that person, inviting them into leadership
and giving them the same task of raising up a successor—or,
even better, a couple of successors, so that the small group
multiplies.

The batons, though simple to make (1-foot lengths of 2"x 2"
oak with the corners trimmed off to form an octagon, var-
nished and then inscribed on one face by a local engraver)
and relatively cheap (about ten bucks each, all told), have
been invaluable in instilling our vision for multiplication of

small group leaders. Very few batons have been dropped in the many years since we started the tradition; small group leaders at UW–Eau Claire have a high degree of ownership of the task of leadership identification and development, I think in large part because of the baton's imagery and symbolism. And in many of our dorms, a single small group leader has multiplied into several small groups. It has been very gratifying for those leaders to graduate, knowing that the small group that they were welcomed into as a freshman and eventually took over leadership of, will continue long after they leave campus, as long as the baton they were entrusted with keeps getting passed.

Whether you ever have a ceremony like this or not isn't the point. The point is simply that small group leaders must reproduce themselves. Whatever the process by which people come into leadership in your context, the role you play as a small group leader in identifying, investing in and developing future leaders is highly significant. Don't drop the baton!

ANYONE CAN LEAD

Úna Lucey-Lee

ABOUT FIVE YEARS AGO, I decided to run a half-marathon. To prepare for the race I followed a training schedule that added mileage progressively through the week and even more on the weekend. I would jog my Saturday "long runs" with my friend Michelle. With a few marathons under her belt, she proved to be helpful in coaching me through the mental and physical hurdles.

During this season, one of Michelle's friends said to me, "I hear from Michelle that you are a runner." I replied, "I like to run but I'm not really a runner." Even though I ran track through adolescence and high school, and running has been a primary form of exercise most of my adult life, I do not have a natural aptitude for long-distance running. Running comes naturally to Michelle. She has the body, the mental toughness, the energy, the focus and the high pain tolerance that I don't have.

The way I saw things, I like to run but Michelle is a runner. When I shared this analogy with a good friend, however, she told me, "Úna, you've run your whole life and you trained and ran a half-marathon. You're a runner!" Well, when you put it that way, I guess I can concede that I am a runner.

This parallels how some people view leadership. You have directed a few events here and there, but you would not call yourself a leader. You recognize a desire to organize projects or people, but you figure everyone shares your interests. You are often recruited to assist leaders, but you do not assume that you should step up and take charge. Some of us assume that leaders are *those other people* with certain personality types, social skills, life experiences and creative ideas— maybe of a certain age and, sometimes, male. Consider me, in this chapter, that friend who is coming alongside you to downplay those qualifications and to highlight the reality that in fact, anyone can lead.

Anyone can lead. I believe this in my heart, and I have had this belief confirmed over many years of training hundreds of leaders. I have led and listened to the discussions about whether leaders are made or whether they are born. But, somehow, the focus on giftedness and the questions on the nurture or nature of leadership seem secondary to the reality that I have experienced in twenty years of leading: *anyone can lead*. Some people will be better at it and will show quicker, more natural aptitude for the nuances of leadership. Some will be more able than many of their peers to naturally attract followers. But if you are willing to work hard and submit yourself to some training you can learn to lead. And whether leadership comes naturally or not, all leaders need to grow into their role. That involves, among other things, developing the godly character necessary for leadership.

WHAT DOES THE BIBLE SAY ABOUT LEADERSHIP?

I rarely hear my family, friends and neighbors refer to themselves as leaders, even if they are a CEO of a big company, the principal of an elementary school or a franchisee in a home-based business. However, in my line of work—campus ministry—the subject of leadership (and leadership identity) is a big one. Among Christians, much of the interest in leadership is fueled by the scriptural references to giftedness.

The Bible is a good resource to learn about leaders and leadership. A quick word search with my handy-dandy computer program reveals that there are some 216 hits for the word *leader(s)*. What is unmistakably clear from the Bible is that there were leaders within the people of God and among the surrounding nations and people groups. There were national leaders but also leaders of tribes, people groups, cities, congregations, armies, synagogues, marauding bands and worship gatherings. In a few instances, God appointed these leaders. According to the Bible, leaders were to serve; they were not to be spoken ill of; their way of life was to be emulated; their authority should be given its due consideration and they should lead with diligence. Jesus is specifically referred to as a leader just once.

I can hear a good friend and a few mentors in my ear saying, "Certainly there are other words to describe leaders." One such substitute word in the Bible is *shepherd*. The earliest biblical reference to the vocation of shepherd is to Abel, who was the second son of Adam and Eve (Genesis 4:2). A shepherd is someone who feeds, protects, raises, cares for and leads sheep. The basic position description of a shepherd is to lead the flock of sheep to tasty grazing and safe shelter. Using this image as a template for leadership, the biblical writers spoke of leaders who either succeed or fail in guiding people. The shepherds in Ezekiel 34 get fat by eating the sheep instead of leading the sheep to good eats. These leaders disbanded the people and let them roam about open to attack instead of gathering them into a protected, safe place. The good news in this storyline is that God is the good shepherd: God will fire these shepherds, gather the people, heal their wounds and develop a safe place for his people to live together. Jesus is the fulfillment of this messianic expectation and the model of the shepherd as leader.

There are other substitute words for *leader* in the Bible, but the major concept behind the biblical teaching is that God is the first leader, the good leader and the best leader. Behind and before each Christian leader is God the Father, Son and Holy Spirit. This truth comes through in Moses' call to leadership in Exodus 3. Moses had a rocky start to life but ended up being raised as family in Pharaoh's home. As a young man, Moses killed an Egyptian man who was beating up a Hebrew man. This failure in basic mediation skills not only tainted his identity as leader of his people but also earned him a death threat from Pharaoh. Moses hit the road in order to preserve his life and found himself pushing sheep around a hill for years—until God got his attention, using a bush that was on fire but was not being reduced to ashes.

At the burning bush, God revealed his plan to lead his people out of oppression and suffering in Egypt and into a quality land and life of their own under his leadership. God intended to send Moses as the emissary to lead God's people out from under Pharaoh's rule but Moses questioned his identity as a leader.

Moses deliberated about his qualifications for this role of leadership. God ignored Moses' question and instead focused on another reality: his presence. To Moses' questions about his own leadership ability, God responded with a promise to be with him. Instead of delineating leadership giftedness and capability or inspiring Moses for the task, God promised his enduring presence.

Moses came back to the promise of God's presence throughout his life. His final speech to the Israelites included numerous reminders that God has promised his presence (Deuteronomy 31:1-6). God's promise to be with him turned out to be the most important aspect of Moses' leadership.

This same promise—that God's presence will go with his people—is repeated at the end of Matthew's Gospel. Jesus commissions his followers to tell the nations about him, and he makes a promise to be with them.

The Great Commission of Matthew 28 hearkens back a passage early in Mark's Gospel: "[Jesus] appointed twelve, whom he also named apostles, *to be with him*, and to be sent out to proclaim the message, and to have authority to cast out demons" (Mark 3:14-15 NRSV, emphasis added). The first call identified in the passage is to be with Jesus. Jesus is *the* leader behind leaders; his apostles' primary task therefore is to be with him. Leaders are to set themselves in God's presence and *then* to move out in leadership.

Fundamental to Jesus' leadership is his desire to bring us into excellent and healthy places where we can grow and mature. We flourish as we live in the presence of God. Equally basic to Jesus' leadership is his objective that we all live with influence in the world. As we step into leadership, we can trust that we will grow there, that we will experience collaborating with God for the sake of his glory.

FEAR OF LEADERSHIP

I have heard numerous objections when I've recruited people into leadership.

"Do I have enough experience?"

"Certainly someone else is better suited."

"How much time will it take?"

"Who will I work with?"

"Maybe I should wait until I understand more of the Bible."

"What happens if I make a mistake?"

"How will this affect my friendship with peers?"

"Am I too old?"

"Am I too young?"

"Someone else must want this job."

"How can I be sure that God wants me to do this?"

Often these questions and statements mask underlying fears, insecurity and anxiety that hinder our participation in the faith-producing task of leadership.

Inexperience may seem like an obstacle to the opportunity to grow personally and serve corporately by leading a small group. If you are considering your first Christian leadership experience then you might wonder if your character fits the bill or if God will actually use you to lead other people. You might be tempted to stay away from leadership because you are *just* a kinesiology major or *just* a mom of two children or *just* a bank teller or *just* a sound technician. Take heart! Some of the first followers of Jesus were *just* fishermen. They were unschooled, ordinary laypeople (Acts 4:13). Through their association with Jesus and other disciples of his, they developed to become some of the first leaders of the church.

DIFFERING EXPECTATIONS AND BARRIERS

The beliefs we bring to leadership can come from our culture, family, experiences, generation and church background. The expectations of leadership within each of these spheres of influence vary, and especially when you are called to lead in a context different from what you are accustomed to, or when you interact with people who view leadership differently, they can become barriers. When I was in college I was asked to

lead a team of my peers that would guide our campus ministry. It just so happens that all the other people on the team
were men. (Someone affectionately called our team "Beauty
and the beasts.") I did not think twice about taking the role
because of my understanding about leaders and teams, but
other students had different opinions about this arrangement.
Many assumed, based on their cultural, family and church experiences, that guys inherently have a hard time being led by
women. There was also some concern about my feeling iso-
lated without another woman with whom I could share the
experience. Some students had never experienced a woman
in this type of leadership and expressed the novelty of this
situation. This student leadership team proved to unearth in
the whole ministry many unspoken ideas about leadership.
Thankfully, none of the guys on the team objected, and we
ended up having a fantastic year together shepherding the
campus ministry toward significant outreach, leadership and
mission on and beyond campus.

Numerous other factors influence our assumptions about
leadership. Some families function by consensus while others
have an evident hierarchy. Some people expect to be led by
people who are older than they are; other people aren't overly
concerned about the age of their leader. Some people value a
hierarchy with clear delineation between who is a leader and
who is not; titles matter. Others prefer flatness in the leadership structure, where the lines are a little blurry between leaders and followers. Some on this end of the spectrum might
reject an official role of leadership simply because it is accompanied with a title of *leader.*

Respect for formal seminary education can sometimes put
undue pressure on lay leadership and squelch opportunities
to lead, and a church's position on women leading men, other

women or at all may be an issue. To grow as leaders, we should check biases and preferences in light of our current context in order to prepare for the opportunity for leadership and the faith risk ahead.

We all approach leadership with numerous values, expectations, ideas and assumptions that we picked up from family, church, experiences, culture and our generation. Some of these are enhancements to leadership while others serve as barriers. As we interact with people different from us, some of our inherent ideas about leadership will emerge. At times, the differences will seem insurmountable and we will question the invitation to leadership or start to develop an exit plan.

Swimmer Natalie du Toit missed her chance to swim in the Sydney, Australia, Olympics in 2000, so she set her sights on Athens in 2004. All of her training and special diet, however, could not protect her from the car that hit her as she left on her moped for school. After four days of rigorous surgery, the doctors were left with only one option: amputation of her left leg at the knee.

Six months after the accident, Natalie was back in the pool. Her determination to swim in the Olympics was stronger than her diminished physical capacity for competition. She had to learn new ways to execute the various swimming strokes. She focused on upper body strength. She competed in international races for the disabled. The whole time she remained focused on the goal of competing in the Beijing Olympics. On August 19, 2008, Natalie dove in the Beijing water for the 10-kilometer open water swim. She was an Olympic swimmer.

The writer of Hebrews uses the image of competitive games, with the crowd cheering on the competitors and the perseverance of the athletes, to teach that the life goal of every follower of Jesus is Jesus himself. We are to look to Jesus. Looking around at the barriers, the limitations and other people serves to distract us from the race itself and Jesus. Leading a small group is a lot of fun, but it can also be grueling, confusing and exhausting work. It is a dynamic activity that keeps us on our toes. Filled with risk, leadership trains us to live into God's presence and seek the leadership of Jesus.

A WARNING TO THOSE WHO LEAD

As we get comfortable in leadership, our inclination to seek God or depend on Jesus might wane. The temptation will be to settle into the plateau and rest. We start looking around at others and comparing our performance to theirs. Unfortunately, one of the byproducts of this stage in leadership is stagnation. This is why it is important to seek Jesus, pursue more training and participate as a follower in your church. It is a fabulous truth of Christian leadership that we have Jesus as our leader, who pours into us blessings, insight and encouragement. It is not his intent or purpose to use us up until he can find another willing victim. He is the Good Shepherd who is leading you and I to good pasture while we are leading small groups. This does not mean that leadership will always be easy or without incident. If we continue to set our sights in Jesus, then he can use the unpleasant leadership experiences to shape our character and develop greater leadership skills.

In addition to not forsaking your relationship with Jesus, do not forsake ongoing leadership training. One of my assignments in campus ministry is to lead Bible discussions with up to twenty-five students. As the leader I am expected to both teach students an inductive method of Bible study and to guide the whole group through a good discussion in the Bible. It was a juggling act to help people learn how to ask good questions of the text as well as to monitor the discussion that would lead to group consensus and application. Whew! During one of these times I asked a colleague of mine to sit in on the group for the express purpose of giving me some feedback on my teaching and discussion-leading skills. I sensed that I needed some help and I could not figure out on my own why some things in the group were not going as well or how to move the group forward toward deeper application.

After a little over an hour the group took a break and my friend and I sat down for me to hear my friend's assessment. After only one hour of watching me lead a group discussion, he had some twenty-eight points of constructive criticism. We talked through all of his input, I asked for clarification where I did not understand, and I came up with a game plan for the next session. I experienced much success in leading the group to better group Bible study as well as application of the Scriptures. My leadership improved because of his feedback.

Whether informal or formal training, leaders need continuing instruction and feedback. It is easy to slack on training either if we feel comfortable in our leadership or if we are experiencing some insecurity. I read leadership books with friends and have attended a seminar on prayer ministry and group intercession. I have called my pastor to ask the meaning of a biblical phrase or to seek his interpretation of a passage. The goal is to nurture a learning posture our whole lives.

My co-leader and I met with someone in our training group as preparation for him to lead Bible study. He came to the meeting having studied the passage and developed a good set of discussion questions. As we were talking through the passage, it became obvious that we had divergent opinions about a few things. The more questions we asked, the more defensive the responses became until he said, "Who do you think you are?" Then it got really awkward.

I took a breath, counted to ten and said, "We are trainers. You are in a training program. We are here to help you succeed in leading a small group for the first time." Part of being a leader is training. As you take on the responsibility of leadership, do not forsake the necessity for input, evaluation and training. One resource for helping me to stay focused on Jesus and to receive instruction on my leadership is to stay connected to a Christian community. Even though I am involved in leadership, it is vital for my growth to be reminded that I am part of a community of believers. I stay connected through attendance, developing real relationships and celebrating key moments in the community. Interacting with people in my church from different generations and socioeconomic backgrounds reminds me that being a small group leader is part of the bigger thing happening among God's people. I can see how my leadership contribution helps expand the kingdom in the neighborhood or the city. The Christian community is also a place where I can participate as a follower of other leaders.

You have decided to lead a small group. You want to lead other people to good and safe pasture where they can receive and grow from God's Word. No training will perfectly prepare you for what actually happens when you lead a small group. However, if you set your sights on Jesus, focusing on the Good Shepherd instead of the surrounding circumstances, then you will receive from him what you need to lead. You would be wise to seek ongoing instruction or specific help to strengthen your leadership, and it is important to stay connected to the community of believers who love you, will pray for you and celebrate with you. You can lead because anyone can lead; everyone who calls Jesus Lord is a partner in his mission and a beneficiary of his Spirit.

APPENDIX

FURTHER RESOURCES FOR SMALL GROUP LEADERS

1. Sample Group Covenant
2. The Communal Discovery Bible Study Method
3. The Hyperlink Bible Study Method
4. Sample Group Meeting Agenda
5. Missional Small Group Evaluation Tool
6. Further Reading for Small Group Leaders

1. SAMPLE GROUP COVENANT

The following is an example of the type of commitment a group may decide to make together before God.

> We, the undersigned, commit before God and to one another to the following:
>
> ### LOVE GOD
>
> *I will pursue spiritual growth through personal Bible study and prayer.*
>
> *I will strive to live a life of integrity and purity.*
>
> ### LOVE ONE ANOTHER
>
> *I will be strive to be Christlike in all my relationships.*
>
> *I will actively seek the opportunity to help a younger Christian grow in their faith.*
>
> *I will reach out to new people at larger group events.*
>
> ### LOVE THE LOST
>
> *I will pray personally (daily) and corporately (at least weekly) for the lost on campus.*
>
> *I will be intentional about befriending non-Christians and sharing my faith with them.*
>
> _____ _____ _____ _____
>
> _____ _____ _____ _____
>
> _____ _____ _____ _____
>
> _____ _____ _____ _____
>
> _____ _____ _____ _____
>
> _____ _____ _____ _____

2. THE COMMUNAL DISCOVERY BIBLE STUDY METHOD

Communal discovery is an offshoot of the inductive method fleshed out in the "Not *Just* Bible Study" chapter. Communal discovery draws its strength from the same roots as the inductive method: *the objective observation, interpretation and application (OIA) of biblical truth.* You are still starting the study with an observation exercise. You are still ending with a summary and applications. The essential difference between the inductive method and communal discovery is that in the interpretation mode the small group leader guides the small group members through the interpretation mode; the small group generates the questions to be discussed. In this way small group members arrive at the truth of a given Scripture passage together.

All the indicators for what do or do not make for good Bible study questions still apply. Communal discovery applies those criteria, however, to observations that the small group members come up with during the small group meeting.

1. Rather than controlling the questions and thus the discussion, small group leaders surrender control of the small group to the Holy Spirit and to the group members.

2. Since the questions are not determined prior to the meeting time, communal discovery allows for multiple outcomes, making things less predictable and more lively.

3. Because the questions are generated by the group, the discussion is directly responsive to what interests group members; the meeting time scratches where the group is itching.

4. Since group members are crafting their own questions of

the Scriptures, much performance pressure is relieved from the small group leader. God's Word—not the group leader's ability to prepare good questions—is at the center of the discussion.

5. Because the group members are being trained to rightly interpret God's Word for themselves, their faith walk and leadership skills deepen.

6. Rather than thinking of the group as belonging to the leader, group members take greater ownership.

At first glance, communal discovery can seem like a free-for-all with little structure. Actually, the small group leader's role in communal discovery is crucial! As with leading an inductive Bible study, your preparation time still involves praying through and feasting on the Word of God for yourself, and interrogating the biblical text to come up with questions. However, in preparing a communal discovery study, you will try to anticipate the questions (helpful *and* unhelpful) that group members may come up with.

1. The criteria for unhelpful and not-so-helpful questions are still the same as in traditional inductive Bible study. At times, small group members may have trouble putting their good insights into question form. Be on the lookout for this, and help small group members to sculpt the raw clay of good insights into a good question about the text. Refer back to the "Not Just a Bible Study" chapter for help in crafting good questions.

2. While you may jot down questions from people in your group, don't feel obligated to put unhelpful questions to the group. This is not as offensive to group members as you might think;

in working through one question the group will often answer one or two less helpful questions. Tell the group up front that you'll only have time for three or four interpretation questions. This helps you to stay within time constraints, and it helps you to more tightly focus on those questions that are most profitable for interrogating the text. Combine overlapping questions into a single clear, tight question. For example, when studying Genesis 2:4-24 you might combine "Why did God create the woman?" with "How are the man and the woman supposed to relate?" into one question: "What do God's motivations for creating the woman tell us about how God wants the man and the woman to relate?"

3. The order of the questions should reflect the natural flow of the passage. In studying John 3:1-21, a question dealing with verses 1-12 (for example, "For Jesus, why is Nicodemus' knowledge insufficient for seeing and entering the kingdom of God?") ought to come before a question pertaining to verses 16-21 (for example, "What is the connection between believing in Jesus and loving the light?").

As in the pure inductive method, you and the group will finish the interpretation time by coming up with a single sentence to summarize the main thrust of the biblical text. Because the entire group has been processing the passage, summary of the text becomes even more crucial in order to draw diverse insights into a beautiful whole.

As in the pure inductive method, a small group leader should have several application questions ready for the small group. However, be ready to adapt your application questions to the insights that the group generates. Also, be prepared to craft entirely new application questions in response to the group's insights.

3. THE HYPERLINK BIBLE STUDY METHOD

All of Scripture is inspired, but it's individual words or phrases that God uses to get our attention and make us think. The words start a thread of thoughts, a trail of interpretations and applications that lead us to a place of comfort, conviction, worship, courage or obedience. In the hyperlink method, you will be taking your group from specific words in the passage through a series of interpretation and application questions to help them engage the passage more deeply.

Classic inductive Bible study methodology was leader-driven with a straightforward structure: ask a couple of observation questions, then ask a couple of interpretation questions, and then ask one or two application questions at the end. Communal discovery shifted the energy for the study onto the group: as group members generate questions for discussion, the small group leader sifts through the questions being brought to the group and decides which ones would be good for the group to tackle.

The Hyperlink method navigates a middle ground between inductive Bible study and communal discovery, maintaining the brilliance of the small group generating the energy for the study while still putting the task of developing good questions (which is a more advanced skill) in the hands of the small group leader. Hyperlink also allows for (and indeed, encourages) application throughout the study.

During a Hyperlink Bible study small group members are given time to study the passage and then are invited to share their observations. The leader has prepared two to five "hyperlinks" ahead of time—a set of interpretation and application questions that developed from observations the leader made of the passage. When a small group member offers an observation that the small group leader has prepared questions for, the leader guides the group through those interpretation and application questions. Once that trail of discussion has run its course through to application, the leader then directs the group back to the Scripture and invites more observations.

What follows is a more fully developed, step-by-step description of how to prepare for and lead a Hyperlink Bible study.

PREPARING FOR A HYPERLINK STUDY

As a leader of a Hyperlink study it is critical that you be open to how the Scripture might speak to you first. We need to approach the Scriptures and the Lord of the Scriptures with humility, ready to be changed personally before we try to change other people. You cannot lead others to wells that you have not drunk from yourself.

So before engaging the group, look over the passage and evaluate: what was one important word or phrase from the text that caused you to step back from the text and to think a little more deeply? Develop one or two interpretation questions and then one or two application questions for this key word or phrase. You've got an observation, then some questions that help make the interpretive steps and then one or two questions that lead to personal application. That's one of your "hyperlinks."

Move on. What are other key words or phrases in this text that were significant to you personally or are obviously important to the point of the passage? Write one or two interpretation questions for each key word or phrase and one or two application questions for those key words or phrases. Each one of those we call a "hyperlink."

At the end of the preparation stage, you should have anywhere from two to five hyperlinks prepared for your Bible study. Figure A.1, from the beginning of Mark 6:30-44 (the feeding of the five thousand), is an example of what your hyperlinks might look like. Before moving on from this stage, you might look over a Bible commentary to make sure that there weren't any critical themes or ideas that you've missed.

After you've prepared your hyperlinks, select one as the "big idea" or main point of the passage. Your group absolutely must discuss this hyperlink if they're going to understand what the author is trying to say. In some passages this is obvious; in other passages the big idea is not as obvious or other themes are equally important. But it's important to note the main idea of a text in order to ensure that your small group covers it before moving on.

The last step of the preparation stage is to write an intro question easy enough for anyone to answer. It should either help people to enter into and get the feel for the passage that they're about to read or set up the main idea of the passage that you will eventually get to.

LEADING A HYPERLINK STUDY

Begin the Bible study section of your small group meeting with your intro question. Not everyone has to answer, but most people should answer the question most of the time.

From there transition to reading the Scripture. I always allow time for people to read the passage silently to themselves. Some folks need more personal time and space to read and engage something; others will quickly skim it and be ready to talk. Be patient with those who need the extra time. I often print out the passages and hand them out, encouraging people to mark them up with pens or colored pencils if that helps them to engage it more deeply on their own.

After several minutes of personal reading, read the text out

1

³⁰The apostles gathered around Jesus and reported to him all they had done and taught.³¹Then, because

2

so many people were coming and going that they did not even have a chance to eat, he said to them,

"Come with me by yourselves to a quiet place and get some rest."

Hyperlink 1: The apostles were sent out by Jesus to heal and teach in the passage just before this and now they return.

Interpretation Question (IQ) 1: What do you think the mood was like here as the apostles re-gathered around Jesus?

IQ 2: What kinds of things do you think the disciples told Jesus about? Do you get the sense that there's some "success" stories happening here?

IQ 3: After several weeks or maybe even months on the road, where does success drive the disciples?

Application Question (AQ): Where does success generally propel you? Back to Jesus or back to yourself? Why?

Hyperlink 2: busy/noisy crowds, Jesus' invitation to get away.

IQ 1: Crowded passage, isn't it? All the introverts in the room are shriveling up as they read it. What do you think the disciples are thinking or feeling in terms of the crowd at this point?

AQ: How many of you have had a day like this in the past week where you had so much to do that you could have easily gone without eating and just kept working?

AQ: How many of you prefer a life that looks like this? How many of you would rather be busy? Why? What might that tell you about the status of your soul?

IQ 2: How do you think the disciples responded to Jesus' invitation?

AQ: How do you respond to Jesus' invitation?

Figure A.1. Hyperlinks from Mark 6:30-44.

loud and then invite people to share whatever struck them from the passage. This is the "observe" part of inductive Bible study. You're asking small group members to offer up their own observations from the text. Sometimes I focus on a portion of the passage: "What did you see in the first half of the chapter?" But "What did you see" is almost always the first question that I ask.

The members then begin to offer their discoveries and thoughts. The leader's job is to "be the Brita" and gently filter out observations that don't accurately reflect the text. (See the chapter "Not *Just* Bible Study" for guidelines on observations.) If you are rude or shut anyone down, people may be unwilling to talk for the rest of the study, so affirm each observation ("That's interesting; why did that strike you?") but then move on, asking the group again for further observations.

When someone touches on one of the words or phrases that you've prepared questions for, they've clicked on your hyperlink! Take the reins of the group and ask your first interpretation question. After some discussion, lead them through the remaining interpretation and application questions that you've prepared for that hyperlink.

There's a very real possibility that someone will offer an important observation that you didn't prepare for. It's important to be open to what the Spirit might want to do that's outside of your plans. If a helpful observation emerges that isn't covered by your pre-arranged hyperlinks, say something like "Wow, I didn't really think much about that, but it seems like it could be important. Let's dig in a little bit there. What do you think X is about?" Once you've led your group through all of your interpretation and application questions and the conversation about a particular hyperlink has come to some sort of conclusion, redirect the group back to the passage: "What else did you all see in the passage?" or perhaps, "Okay, let's move on to the next part of the chapter. What struck you about these next verses?"

Keep an eye on your primary hyperlink. If you haven't hit on it by the second or third conversation, then you might need to make the observation yourself and then immediately ask the interpretation question that you've prepared for it: "I thought it was interesting that Jesus said X in verse 30. Why do you think he said that?"

After three or four hyperlink conversations (fewer if the conversations have been substantive) you should close up with a short summary and a prayer.

4. SAMPLE GROUP MEETING AGENDA

The following is a sample structure for preparing to lead a small group meeting.

Biblical Passage/Text to Be Studied:

Main Point/Central Truth of Passage:

Leader's "Must-Have" Questions:

Four Components to Be Addressed During Meeting:

Prayer/Worship:

    Nurturing/Developing Disciples:

    Community/Relationship Building:

    Mission/Outreach:

Opening Prayer:

Read Passage Aloud (optional):

Intro/Background Info (5 min):

Creative Entry Idea (10 min):

Private Observations and Questions (10 min):

Group Observations and Questions (10 min):

Leader's observations:	Group's observations:
Leader's questions:	Group's questions:

Discussion (20 min):

Summary of Main Point/Central Truth (5 min):

Application (10 min):

5. MISSIONAL SMALL GROUP EVALUATION TOOL

This tool, adapted slightly from Scott Bockstruck's design, helps small groups evaluate how missional they are. Rank your small group in the categories found in table A.1 (p. 178), based on the assessment questions under each heading (1 = never 2 = rarely 3 = sometimes 4 = often 5 = consistently). Total the rankings for each category and divide by 10 to get the median rank. Then plot your median rankings on the graph in figure A.2.

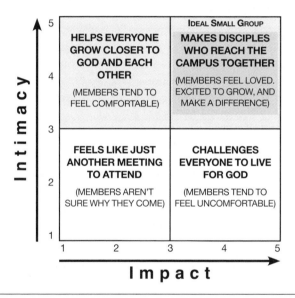

Figure A.2.

Table A.1.

INTIMACY (with God and one another)	Rank
Group members spend time with each other outside of the meeting.	
The group is led to encounter the text effectively before attempting to discern its meaning.	
There is a level of self-disclosure in the prayer requests of members that goes well beyond family health issues and tests.	
Everyone contributes equally in the Bible study, as opposed to a few people who seem to answer every question.	
Group members seem to remember each other's prayer requests and check in regarding them.	
The group focuses on who God is and responds together in worship when they gather.	
The group makes occasions to celebrate with each other.	
Members leave each meeting with a solid grasp of the central point of the Bible passage that was studied.	
Group worship times are led with creativity and diversity.	
Prayer times seem to flow naturally from what the group is experiencing and are not just an allotted time of the meeting.	
Total Score for Intimacy: **Median Ranking for Intimacy (Total Score Divided by 10):**	
IMPACT (on campus and personally)	Rank
A group member could easily describe what specific community the group has been called to (e.g., art students, single mothers).	
The group reaches out to this community by serving them and proclaiming God's love.	
Group members invite new people to join them or check out the group.	
The group prays passionately for the community it's been called to.	
Members leave the meeting each week with concrete applications that can be lived out that week.	
The group responds together as a community to what a Bible passage is teaching.	
Group members are intentionally being invested in by the leaders or older members.	
Group members hold each other accountable to the resolutions they make.	
Potential leaders are being identified and invested in toward raising up new leaders.	
Potential leaders are given chances to practice leading.	
Total Score for Impact: **Median Ranking for Impact (Total Score Divided by 10):**	

6. FURTHER READING FOR SMALL GROUP LEADERS

If you want a classic, all-time favorite on a deeply Christian understanding about community, check out Deitrich Bonhoeffer's *Life Together* (San Francisco: Harper, 1978). Surprisingly short and easy to read, it packs a tremendous punch.

For one of the most comprehensive and thoroughgoing books on how community works best to encourage spiritual growth, check out *How People Grow* by Henry Cloud and John Townsend (Grand Rapids: Zondervan, 2004).

Another good book about community dynamics and spiritual growth is *The Safest Place on Earth* by Larry Crabb (Nashville: Thomas Nelson, 1999).

To learn more about coming alongside people and shepherding them, see *Sacred Companions* by David Benner (Downers Grove, Ill.: InterVarsity Press, 2004).

There are a number of good books about Bible study, but a perennial favorite is *How to Read the Bible for All Its Worth* by Gordon Fee and Doug Stuart (Grand Rapids: Zondervan, 2003).

More insights into leading communal discovery Bible studies can be found at <www.intervarsity.org/biblestu/page/communal-discovery-method>.

Bob Grahmann's comprehensive communal discovery leader's guide can be downloaded at <www.intervarsity.org/biblestu/communal/leading_a_communal_discovery_bible_study.pdf>.

Recent history's definitive book on prayer is Richard Foster's *Prayer: Finding the Heart's True Home* (San Francisco: HarperOne, 1992). It can be read chapter by chapter as a powerful weekly exercise for a small group.